Prentice-Hall, Inc., Englewood Cliffs, N.J.

Urbanization in Newly Developing Countries

GERALD BREESE Bureau of Urban Research
Princeton University

Library of Congress Catalog Card No.: 66-20633

Current printing (last digit):

10 9 8 7 6 5 4 3

Printed in the United States of America
C-93919(C) C-93918(P)

FOR ALICE JANETTE
ADELE, JAY, DANA, AND BRINDA
WHO SHARED AND CARE

PRENTICE-HALL INTERNATIONAL, INC.
London

PRENTICE-HALL OF AUSTRALIA, PTY. LTD.
Sydney

PRENTICE-HALL OF CANADA, LTD.
Toronto

PRENTICE-HALL OF INDIA (PRIVATE) LTD.
New Delhi

PRENTICE-HALL OF JAPAN, INC.
Tokyo

WILBERT E. MOORE / NEIL J. SMELSER Editors

Modernization of Traditional Societies Series

The twentieth century will be called many things by future historians—the Age of Global War, perhaps, the Age of Mass Society, the Age of the Psychoanalytic Revolution, to name a few possibilities. One name that historians certainly will not fail to give our century is the Age of the New Nation. For, evidently, the convulsive emergence of the colonies into independence and their subsequent struggle to join the ranks of the prosperous, powerful, and peaceful is the most remarkable revolution of our time. Taking the world as a whole, men are now preoccupied with no subject more than they are with the travail of the New Nations.

The world of the social sciences has been studying the pace of social change in these newly emergent areas, and from time to time has been engaging in technical assistance and even in the giving of advice on high levels of social strategy. Little of this effort has reached publicly accessible form. Though technical treatises abound, and isolated, journalistic reports of distinctly exotic countries are not wanting, college curricula have scarcely reflected either the scientific endeavors or the world-wide revolutions in technology and in political affairs.

This series on "Modernization of Traditional Societies" is designed to inform scholars, students, and citizens about the way quiet places have come alive, and to introduce at long last materials on

EDITORIAL FOREWORD

the contemporary character of

developing areas into college curricula for the thought leaders of the near future. To these ends we have assembled experts over the range of the social sciences and over the range of the areas of the underdeveloped and newly developing sections of the earth that were once troublesome only to themselves.

We are proud to be participants in this series, and proud to offer each of its volumes to the literate world, with the hope that that world may increase, prosper, think, and decide wisely.

WILBERT E. MOORE
NEIL J. SMELSER

PREFACE

This book is intended to serve as an introductory discussion of urbanization in the modernization process of newly developing countries. It is exploratory in prospect and it includes, generally by implication, suggestions for needed new research.

Among the difficulties in studying this subject is that not all countries in the world are at the same level of urbanization and development; thus comparisons are complicated. Further, it is occasionally necessary to make tentative generalizations since equally reliable data are not available for all countries. Future revisions must be expected for virtually all observations made here.

No attempt is made to summarize the vast amount of literature in the form of monographs, surveys, theoretical and practical projects, and study reports on this subject because of space limitations. The best of this literature merits reading, rather than dismissal by abstract or summary.

A source book presenting data and research findings dealing with urbanization in newly developing countries is being prepared. It is hoped that this will supplement the present study.

We make no attempt to be exhaustive, not only because of the lack of space but also because it is impossible for any one person to speak expertly on all dimensions of the subject.

The global title may be somewhat

misleading, for the book is certainly only peripherally concerned with the so-called population explosion in the world. It deals with Anglo-European urbanization in Europe, Great Britain, the United States, and Canada only insofar as they serve as models for urbanization elsewhere.

There is no detailed history of specific cities, for special monographs would be required and are in the process of being written.

This book is concerned not with unique cases but with the more commonly observable features of urbanization outside Anglo-European society. Although the full range of urbanization is kept in mind, cities of all sizes are not explored. Rather, the focus is on major examples of urbanization in newly developing countries.

The subject is a vast one, so vast it induces a genuine feeling of humility. The new world of urban living lies before hundreds of millions and more. It is hoped this introduction will serve as an invitation to explore their future—and ours as it is related to it—in further detail.

This book is based on extended study of the literature on urbanization and upon firsthand field examination of most of the large urban areas in Europe, nearly all of Africa, much of the Middle East, the Indian subcontinent, and southeast Asia eastward to Japan.

Every student is the conscious or unconscious beneficiary of all extant research in his field of interest. Over the years the play and interplay, the modification, the replacement of one bit of information by another, and the gradual emergence of new constellations of knowledge about urbanization blur origins and it becomes impossible to sort out which ideas are one's own and which have come from others. Thus a blanket acknowledgment is my only recourse, no matter how inadequate it may be.

I welcome this occasion to thank the myriad urbanization scholars and also Neil J. Smelser and Wilbert E. Moore, the editors of this series, particularly the latter for his invitation to participate and for much helpful advice and assistance. Profound thanks are offered to my wife, Alice Janette, and to our children who accompanied us on endless journeys upon the globe. I am grateful to Princeton University's Bureau of Urban Research, and especially to the assistant director, Dorothy E. Whiteman, for her interest and extraordinary editorial and bibliographical skills.

In some respects, I thank, above all, the inhabitants of urban areas throughout the world who allowed me to walk among them with what I trust were perceptive as well as interested and sympathetic eyes.

GERALD BREESE

Contents

When does this day begin? Is it with the corner baker who draws the night's first loaves of bread from the oven which send forth an aroma that enlivens neighbors who have money to buy some, but further shrinks the stomachs of the poor who will go hungry? Does it begin with the villager who, having traveled all night by cart, finally reaches the market place to bargain off his poor load of produce and then, in the quiet darkness, heads his bullock homeward and falls asleep exhausted? Is it when a woman rises from the darkness of her mat, slings her baby on her hip, and fashions an eye-stinging fire from some mixed straw and dry dung?

It takes an early morning riser indeed to establish the beginning of the day in a city not yet committed to Anglo-European ways. Is it when a muezzin sounds his first call to prayer from the nearest minaret? Or is it when the cabinet minister or business executive hears outside his windows the click of gardeners cutting flowers for the day and rises to don his carefully valeted clothes, to savor his chilled mango, and later to step into his chauffeured limousine? Or is it when the homeless sidewalk sleeper is roused from his fitful aching slumber by the prod of a *lathi* and told by police to be on his way? Or is it when the tardy nightsoil gatherer heads his untouchable self for the fields and offends the nostrils of the *busti*

Prologue

dweller silently walking to his daily hod-carrying at a construction site?

Whatever the beginning point, the day is born and moves relentlessly to its end. The morning pall of acrid smoke from countless fires is washed away by a monsoon storm or lost in the shimmering heat. Shutters are removed from shop windows, beggars take up their stands, clerks wheel by in swarms of cycles, myriad laborers pad along their weary routes carrying their heavy burdens, straining buses lurch from side to side as they wend their way through congested arteries, coffee and tea are made and drunk, business transpires, and policies are determined in legislatures.

The city in newly developing countries is a study in contrast of old and new, survivals of rural past and innovations from the West. This mixture is apparent not only in what one sees, but also within the inhabitants of such cities.

What does the eye see here?

It sees human beasts of burden being shouldered aside by massive trucks. It sees a new IBM machine resplendently exposed on its packing case pallet being delivered from dock to skyscraper by bullock cart.

It sees the teeming, sweltering warrens, where only the poorest dwell, adjoining luxurious villas where the only noise comes from an air-conditioner or splashing in a pool. It sees how the loud clap from supersonic flight that penetrates the carpeted mosque bestirs the *guru* sitting cross-legged in an archway. It sees the postures and rituals of traditional wedding ceremonies occurring before attendants who watched an American boudoir film at the cinema the day before. It sees the lilting step inspired by the transistor music mysteriously emanating from beneath the flowing *galabeya* of the man on the sidewalk.

It sees the jumble of camel carts, Mercedes trucks, rickshas, decrepit taxis, *sadhus* in saffron, and police in jeeps on every thoroughfare. It sees the snarling bulldozer ripping away at the earth to provide a foundation for the next skyscraper. It sees the sidewalk vendor in front of the Kingsway air-conditioned department store. It sees the seemingly chaotic convolution of alleys and lanes in the old city within sight of broad Haussmann-like avenues lined with contemporary architecture rising from the surrounding parking lots.

It sees vultures picking quarrelsomely at offal next door to a Cook's Tour point of interest thronged with camera-laden travelers. It sees flamboyantly dressed women in saris shopping for European-style dresses. It sees nuclear research installations, air-conditioned against the acrid fumes of dung-stoked cooking fires. It sees the newly arrived young migrant as he clambers down from atop a lorry load of vegetables, windblown and thirsty from the ride that has brought him to the city, wondering just where and how to start making his way.

It sees the low-caste Indian slip into the ranks of factory workers, finally on the way to an escape from an inherited status. It sees the bright eyes of anticipation in the first-generation university student sampling knowledge hitherto beyond the interest and access of his forebears. It sees the halting but increasingly exploratory search for a mate of one's own choosing, not a mate prescribed by the limits of family contacts or village population. It sees the unfettering of a custom-bound youth in "the city air which makes one free," even though perhaps untutored to the reality that one may slip into the miasma of urban poverty; there is at least a chance that he may end otherwise, his potential realized.

It sees the other hundreds of thousands of people similar to that youth: the many who have been in the city longer with varying success, some resigned, some few flourishing beyond their greatest dreams.

These things are far from unique to a particular country. Wherever one goes, whichever country one examines, one finds the undeniable evidence of urbanization, a virtually universal phenomenon.

SOME MATTERS OF DEFINITION

There were large agglomerations in the ancient world, even some with high density. The latter, however, were structurally more like massed villages, rather than urban, in the sense with which we are now familiar. Generally these examples of urbanization in newly developing countries are associated with industrialization, though the degree of association, especially the causal degree of association, has varied greatly or even not existed. For example, in some cases rather large urban areas have developed which were not industrial in character, but were colonial, administrative, or marketing centers developed by the initiative of foreigners; in other words, these areas were characterized by a kind of urbanization that was externally imposed.

Urbanization, Detribalization, and Stabilization

Since we are dealing here with urbanization in newly developing countries, it is perhaps desirable to clarify the distinctions among the terms *urbanization, detribalization,* and *stabilization,* since there is considerable confusion in the use of these terms. J. Clyde Mitchell points out that these terms are sometimes used interchangeably, which arises, perhaps, from an unrecognized assumption which is an implicit value judgment as to what has taken place. Mitchell refers to urbanization as being the process of becoming urban, moving to cities, changing from agriculture to other pursuits common to cities, and corresponding changing of behavior patterns. Mitchell sees detribalization as being constituted of two different kinds of factors: (1) demographic, in which reference may be made to differences in age and sex characteristics between rural and urban areas, sometimes referring to the movement from tribal areas into urban, and (2) sociological, such as undertaking residence away from the area of the chief to whom allegiance is owed, severing obligations and relationships with the chief, and becoming economically independent from rural relatives. Mitchell suggests that the term stabilization be reserved for the settled urban residence of migrants. This, of course, begs the question as to when a migrant becomes a resident, and to this we shall return later. He prefers to use the word urbanization to describe the development of modes and standards of behavior peculiar to urban areas. Mitchell defines detribalization, on the other hand, as "the general change from tribal to western standards of behavior"; however, he urges that this word not be used.[1]

Other Important Terms

The three most important terms to have clearly defined are *urbanization, industrialization,* and *newly developing* or *modernizing* countries. The succeeding chapter shows that the amount and kind of urbanization in newly developing areas of the world vary from country to country. Some countries have a very low percentage of urban population, but the total number involved may be very large. Other countries have a relatively small population with a very high percentage classified as urban.

In studying urbanization in newly or rapidly developing countries, it is important to divest oneself of the Western image of urbanization. This process is absolutely mandatory, though difficult. For example, it is important to imagine a kind of urbanization in which there may be very little modern transportation, as in the case of a city in India with a population of more than 2,000,000 in which the number of automotive vehicles—cars, trucks, and buses—amounts to only 20,000. This is in very great contrast to the Western urbanization with which we are familiar.

The vast majority of such urban populations in newly developing countries will consist of recent migrants to the city, in contrast to Western cities. Most of these migrants will have no handle on their society, *i.e.,* they will have no means to achieve control of the environ-

[1] J. Clyde Mitchell, "Urbanization, Detribalization, and Stabilization in Southern Africa: A Problem of Definition and Measurement," report of the International African Institute, London. Prepared under the auspices of UNESCO, *Social Implications of Industrialization and Urbanization in Africa South of the Sahara* (Paris: UNESCO, 1956), pp. 693ff. (hereafter referred to as UNESCO, *Africa South of the Sahara*).

ment in which they are living. This is in complete contrast to Western forms of urbanization where delegative, representative governments have been developed to the point where by means of such representation, as well as by pressure group activities, the ordinary citizen can make some impact on the environment in which he lives.

And, as we shall see, the vast majority of urban populations in newly developing countries has a quite different level of living from that found in urbanized, Western countries.

Subsistence Urbanization

The familiar concept of *subsistence agriculture* connotes a level of living derived from agricultural production on which one can barely exist and which therefore permits no surplus to be exported, sold, or otherwise disposed of for funds to improve the standard of living. There is a kind of parallel subsistence in the urbanization of many newly developing countries. It is useful, therefore, to introduce the new term *subsistence urbanization*. This implies urbanization in which the ordinary citizen has only the bare necessities, and sometimes not even those, for survival in the urban environment. This is not a very complimentary description of urbanization in newly developing or modernizing countries, but the evidence seems to indicate that the vast majority of people in such places does indeed live on a level of subsistence urbanization. The readily observable evidence, in addition to available data of the conditions in which the residents live, consists of their generally very low level of housing, their diet, the clothing that they can afford to buy, and what amenities of life are available to them. This is an urbanization of very high density, of individuals living under conditions that may be even worse than the rural areas from which they have come, of not having available the kinds of work or the means of support which will permit them to do more than merely survive.

Industrialization

The term industrialization has frequently been confused or used interchangeably with urbanization. In some parts of the world industrialization and urbanization have gone hand in hand and have developed together. Elsewhere industrialization has been very recent. In still other countries, urbanization and industrialization are both still very much in the process of developing, and one may eventually exceed the other. It is possible, as was true in the very early appearance of large cities in China, for example, to have large agglomerations of people at relatively high densities without industrialization; it is also possible to have industrialization without a high level of urbanization. The terms are not interchangeable. Furthermore, there is no necessary correlation, causally speaking, between industrialization and urbanization, though they do tend to take place at much the same time. In countries where this does not occur, leaders make every effort to introduce industrialization at as rapid a pace as possible to provide employment for the great number of persons flocking to large cities. The excess of urbanization over industrialization that makes it possible to provide employment for all persons coming to urban areas is, in fact, what sometimes leads to *overurbanization,* which will be discussed later.

Newly Developing Countries

The concept of newly developing or modernizing countries must also be understood. Such countries may have a relatively low, or even a high, rate of urbanization. Caution must be exercised not to oversimplify the differences between a rapidly—as against a slowly—developing country. There are obviously many different stages or levels of development which vary from country to country and from aspect to aspect of the system itself. The differentials in the rate of development for different sectors of the economy and of the society are all highly variable. A particular aspect of change may occur very rapidly and then halt while other aspects of the society catch up with it, and then these different aspects may again develop at different rates.

It is important to make clear that designating a country as newly developing or *rapidly developing* refers only to the fact that it is "underdeveloped" in comparison with Western culture. The indigenous social and economic organization of many non-Western cultures may be very complex. Perhaps it is only in the process of superimposing Western standards on another culture that a country may be classified as relatively underdeveloped.

It is sometimes helpful to replace the term newly developing country with modernizing country in the sense referred to by Wilbert E. Moore as "the total transformation of a traditional or pre-modern society into the types of technology and associated social organization that characterize the 'advanced' economically prosperous, and relatively politically stable nations of the Western world." [2] Moore sees the process of modernization as most commonly approached in terms of economic development or, more generally, industrialization.

[2] Wilbert E. Moore, *Social Change* (Englewood Cliffs, N. J.: Prentice-Hall, Inc., 1963), p. 89.

In this connection, Moore further points out a helpful differentiation between traditional societies and modern societies, noting that one must be very cautious in the use of dichotomies that oversimplify, but do not necessarily clarify, differences. Moore refers to the major characteristics of traditional societies as those displaying an emphasis on affectivity, consensus (mechanical solidarity), and informal controls, in contrast with our usual conception of modern society as involving a high order of impersonality, interdependent specialization (organic solidarity), and formal controls over behavior.[3] Since these matters have been explored elsewhere, their definitions are not pursued here.

If industrialization can be said to have been the first great and continuing revolution in recent times, then certainly the world's second great recent and continuing revolution is urbanization.

The undeniable evidence is that the urbanization in newly developing countries is appearing not only in larger magnitudes but in bigger and bigger units, that is, not only is there more and more urban population but there are also more places which are urban and they are becoming larger and larger.[4]

Although Anglo-European countries have by no means resolved all of the problems of urbanization in their domains, it nevertheless appears evident that world-wide urbanization is taking place in a peculiar context; this raises many questions and fails to resolve many issues. It has been said:

> This is a world-wide phenomenon. . . . The impact of urban growth may be even greater in the underdeveloped countries than in the industrialized nations, for it is occurring on top of a mass of other problems which North Americans and Europeans have to some degree already solved: political stability, independence, relative economic stability, decent living standards, and orderly and flexible social structure. This is a truly new international frontier of great importance.[5]

Thus David E. Lilienthal called attention to the many ramifications of the new kind of urbanization being superimposed upon and developing within a different context from the urbanization with which we are already familiar.

[3] Wilbert E. Moore, at Inter-American Sociology Seminar, Princeton University (September 1962), reported in "Introduction: Social Change and Comparative Studies," *International Social Science Journal,* **15** (1963), 522. (Parentheses are from personal letter of July 19, 1965.)

[4] See Chap. One, "The Scale and Pace of Urbanization," following.

[5] David E. Lilienthal, *Metropolitan Area Problems,* **5** (May–June 1962), 5.

APPROACH TO THE SUBJECT

It is appropriate at this point to specify the approach and contents of this consideration of urbanization as part of a series on the modernization of traditional societies.

Chapter One is devoted to the scale and pace of urbanization, examining very briefly where, outside Anglo-Europe, urbanization is taking place and the pattern vis-à-vis traditional societies: To what extent do these phenomena exist? What percentages of the world population are involved? What are the variations from place to place and the ranges of urbanization to date? What about the uneven rates of urbanization in different parts of the world? Following this, a brief retrospective section considers the "then" and "now," a brief review of the emergence of cities related to traditional societies, both indigenous urbanization and urbanization under colonial influence, and as presently conceived, to lend some perspective and remove some misconceptions.

Chapter Two is devoted to both the role of the city in newly developing countries and the kinds and characteristics of emerging urbanization, with some notes on the variety and morphology of cities in newly developing countries. Particular attention is directed to the question of why the city exists. This is first examined through time, with the city emerging in most cases as a market *extraordinaire,* as a point of contact with the outside world. It may have been a locus of power for government and economic and political operations, an agency and diffusion point of social change from the rural pattern, or it may have served as a receptacle for the highest talent as well as for those most in need and those most readily led, for manpower in the country, and for investment funds.

The existing urban areas are studied in terms of their special role, partly a combination of the retention of earlier functions; the development of commercial, foreign aid, and international service activities which have gravitated toward them; and their serving as a magnet for national population, sometimes above the capacity of the city to employ, house, service, feed, and educate.

Certain policy implications of these changes in the role of the city are investigated, with particular attention being paid to the cultural stresses and strains in the confrontation of the indigenous population with the imported human potpourri.

The typology of urban areas is discussed, and the origins of variations found in urbanization in newly developing countries are noted, with special focus on the primate city case. Further permutations and combinations by function, size, and age of rapidly urbanizing areas are analyzed, and cities in less- and well-developed countries are compared and contrasted by type. This is followed by detailed discussion of the relationship between industrialization and urbanization in developing countries. The final part of Chapter Two turns to the question of *urban morphology,* that is, a cross-sectional or static view of the urban area in newly developing countries at the present time. Matters of site and situation, size and scale, and existence and relationship of functional areas, and the general image of the city in terms of pattern and profile are reviewed.

Chapter Three is concerned with the inhabitants of these newly developing urban areas. The contrast between the familiar Western urbanization and the urbanization occurring in these newly developing areas is likely to be so strong that a familiarity with the Western patterns is grossly inadequate preparation for comprehending the full gamut of urban society in newly modernizing countries.

Many questions emerge with reference to inhabitants. Who are they? What are their numbers and their characteristics? What are their origins, why did they come to the particular urban area, how did they receive their first information about it, and how did they manage to reach it? How does this compare at the present time with earlier patterns of migration, are there any laws of migration to urban areas under these circumstances, is there any selectivity in the migrating population?

Various internal and temporal changes are discussed, particularly in terms of physical and social mobility as well as in terms of seasonal and other variations. Special attention is devoted to the role of the individual, the family, and other units, including a detailed discussion of group organization.

Various institutional phenomena in rapid urbanization are next examined, particularly with relation to religion, education, and government. Finally, in a general overview, these phenomena are examined in one comprehensive picture and matters such as rural transplants and survivals, the differences between expectation and achievement, the alternatives to the prevailing features of urbanization, and the prospect that derives from these considerations are discussed.

Whereas in Chapter Two the static city is examined, in Chapter Four attention is drawn to the developing city in rapidly growing countries. Here, even more than elsewhere, urban areas are seen to be in flux, now imperceptibly, now violently changing, seemingly defying all attempts at prediction. Attention is first directed to growth patterns, followed by a consideration of the ecological processes observable in the development of the city, exploring some of the knowns and unknowns in the internal functional relationships in newly developing urban areas.

These subjects involve an understanding of land use, land values, and land ownership, and are supported by a discussion of the mechanics of urban life, and the requirements and capabilities of urban facilities and services.

Finally, the developing city is seen in the context of urban planning insofar as it exists in the newly developing countries. The nature of the problem, the status of planning for urbanization in theory and practice, and the related questions of policy are analyzed.

The final chapter is devoted to a brief discussion of the shape of things to come, including an inquiry into whether the past characteristics of urbanization in newly developing countries can be projected into the future, or whether future urbanization in modernizing countries will have quite different features from those that predominate today. Very closely related to this question is the whole matter of overurbanization, which is explored in some detail. Special attention is devoted to a consideration of the relationship of the city to the country. Finally, an effort is made at prediction—a review of trends with implications for the future.

DATA LIMITS AND TERMS OF REFERENCE

It is necessary to observe the limitations affecting the study of urbanization in newly developing countries. Although there exist some excellent monographs and special studies of rapidly developing cities in newly growing countries, data are very spotty and differential from one country to another and from one part of the world to another.[6] The result is that there is a great deal of dependence on what exists in lieu of comprehensive and balanced availability of information concerning urban areas in all parts of the world. This is a caveat which is regrettable, but a limit within which we have to work. It follows that most of the data that can be adduced to support a particular point of view are likely to come from the larger rather than the smaller cities in newly developing countries, since it is in general true that the larger the city the more readily data are available for that city and the more special studies that will have been made. However, these limitations are hopefully compensated for by firsthand observation of a rather wide range of urbanization throughout the world.

One matter remains to be discussed in greater detail: the definition of

[6] See fn. 1, p. 14.

urban, to which incidental reference was made above. National definitions of what is urban differ greatly. For example, one nation's definition of urban includes places having a few hundred population; another nation may require a place to have several thousand population before it is designated as urban. For the sake of convenience, and since it is now a commonly accepted practice, this book will utilize an arbitrary minimum of 20,000 population as necessary for designating a place as urban. Also, unless specifically noted otherwise, the terms *urban area* and *city* will be used interchangeably, and will not imply a politically separable unit, but an urbanized area as a whole.

WORLD POPULATION CHANGES

In some respects the individual must become a mere integer within very large numbers when discussing the scale and pace of urbanization. This is inevitable in both a real and a symbolic sense: real in terms of "rubbing elbows" with the vast numbers of people who live in urban areas; symbolic in terms of both the range and the intensity of interdependence on fellow residents.

These phenomena vary from city to city. There is a significant difference in urban experience for those living in a city with a population of 20,000, 200,000, or 2,000,000. There are also significant differences in living in a city which has had a long rather than a short history, regardless of the city size.

Quantities and rates of growth contribute to an understanding of urbanization, and the propensity to classify and categorize urban areas for this purpose is enhanced by access to ample, reliable data. Unfortunately, certain reservations must be kept in mind when dealing with such data for newly developing countries: with but a few exceptions, both the frequency and the sophistication of census-taking in most of these countries require much improvement. Nevertheless, some useful data exist which, when used with restraint in view of their limitations, reveal the general features of urbanization.

CHAPTER ONE

The Scale and Pace of Urbanization

A great portion of the world's inhabitants

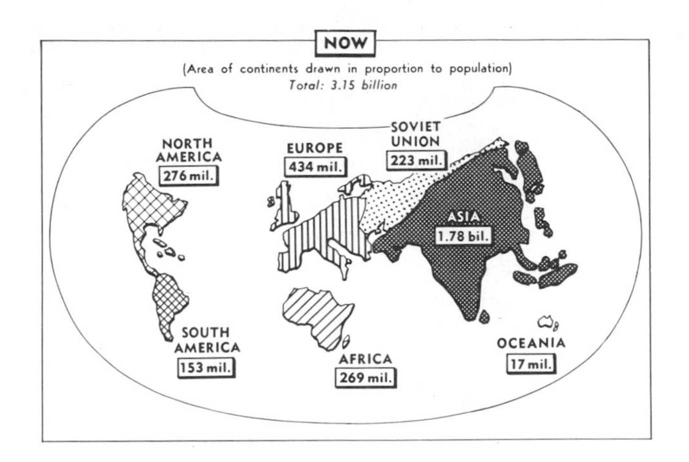

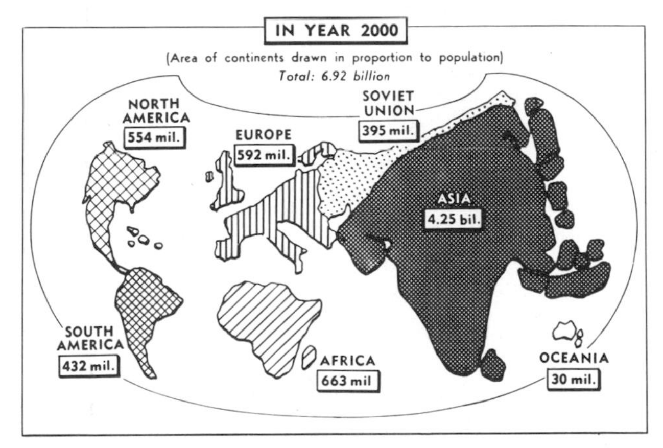

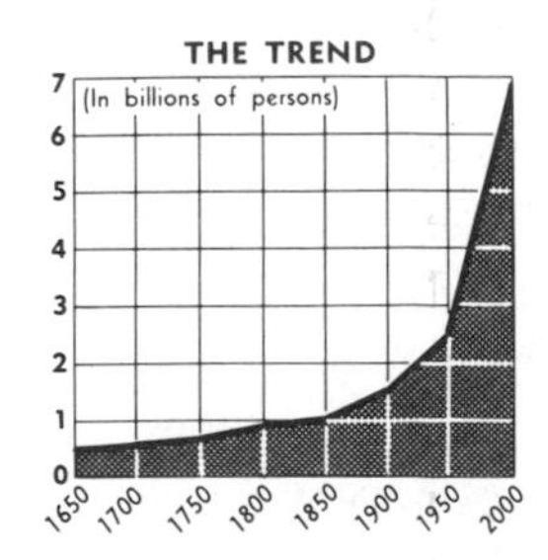

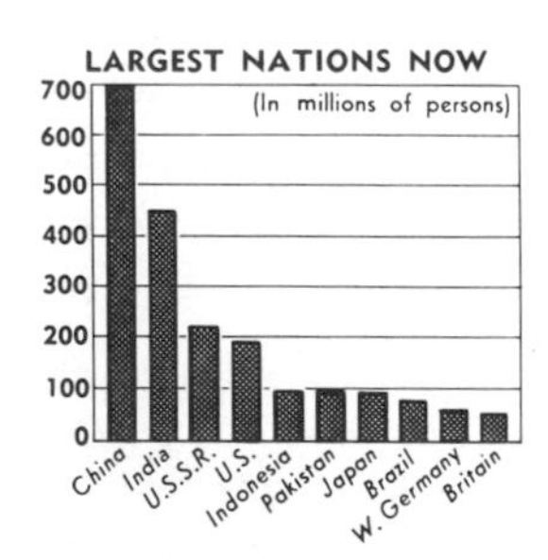

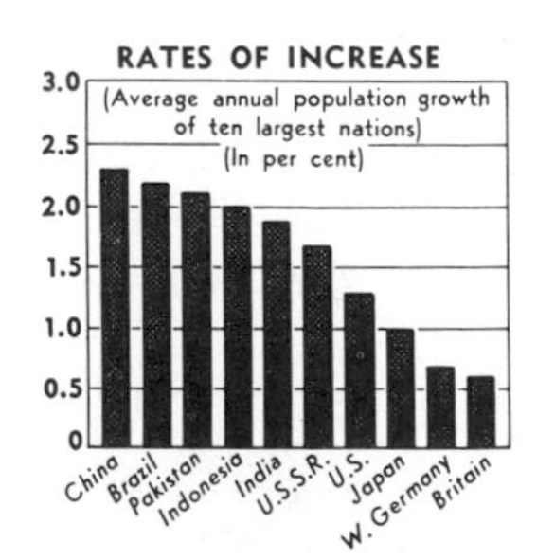

FIGURE 1

World Population—The Picture Now and a Look toward 2000

Source: Copyright 1963 by The New York Times Company. Reprinted by permission.

are gradually becoming accustomed to the fact—although its full significance is seldom understood—that global population is at least going to double before 2000 (see Figure 1). Not yet comprehended, however, is the fact that at the same time a substantial increase in world-wide urbanization is anticipated. It is the purpose of this chapter to review, necessarily briefly and from already published sources,[1] where in the world—outside Anglo-Europe—urbanization is taking place, especially in newly developing countries. The following details will be examined: the percentage of the world population involved in urbanization, the variations of urbanization from place to place, the ranges in urbanization to date, and the uneven rates of urbanization together with causes and consequences, coincidences, and relationships.

Some visual impression of the present pattern of world urbanization, as compared with the existing distribution of *total* world population, is suggested in Figure 2. The first map shows the percentages of the total population living in cities of 100,000 or more, subdivided into three categories. The second map shows various parts of the world drawn to their proportion of population scale and suggests the potential for urban development. The subject of potential urban development is discussed in Chapter Five. Here we will examine the growth and extent of urbanization, with particular reference to newly developing countries, and suggest the variations and ranges of urban development that have taken place up to this point.

Some idea of the rate at which urbanization has been proceeding is suggested in the 1957 United Nations *Report on the World Social Situation,* which notes that:

> Between 1800 and 1950, the population of the world living in cities with 20,000 or more inhabitants increased from about 21.7 million to 502.2 million, expanding 23 times in 150 years, while the total world population expanded about 2.6 times in the same period; 2.4 per cent of the world's population lived in urban centers of 20,000 or more in 1800, 20.9 per cent in 1950.[2]

[1] Throughout the book it will be apparent that the author has depended on the work of the following individuals and organizations who have done pioneering work in the preparation of data dealing with urbanization throughout the world. Full citation of each source is given at the first point of use: Kingsley Davis and Hilda Hertz; International Urban Research, University of California; UNESCO; United Nations; Homer Hoyt; and International Statistical Institute.

[2] United Nations Secretariat, Bureau of Social Affairs, in cooperation with International Labor Office, Food and Agriculture Organization, UNESCO, and World Health Organization, *Report on the World Social Situation Including Studies of Urbanization in Underdeveloped Areas* (New York: United Nations, 1957), p. 113 (hereafter referred to as: UN, *World Social Situation: 1957*). The source of the data indicated in this quotation is noted as "based largely on estimates prepared by Kingsley Davis and Hilda Hertz, 'Patterns of World Urbanization.'" See also "World and Asian Urbanization in Relation to Economic Development and Social Change," by Philip M. Hauser, *rapporteur* for the joint UN/UNESCO seminar *Urbanization in the ECAFE Region,* issued as E/CN.11/URB/10, July 18, 1956.

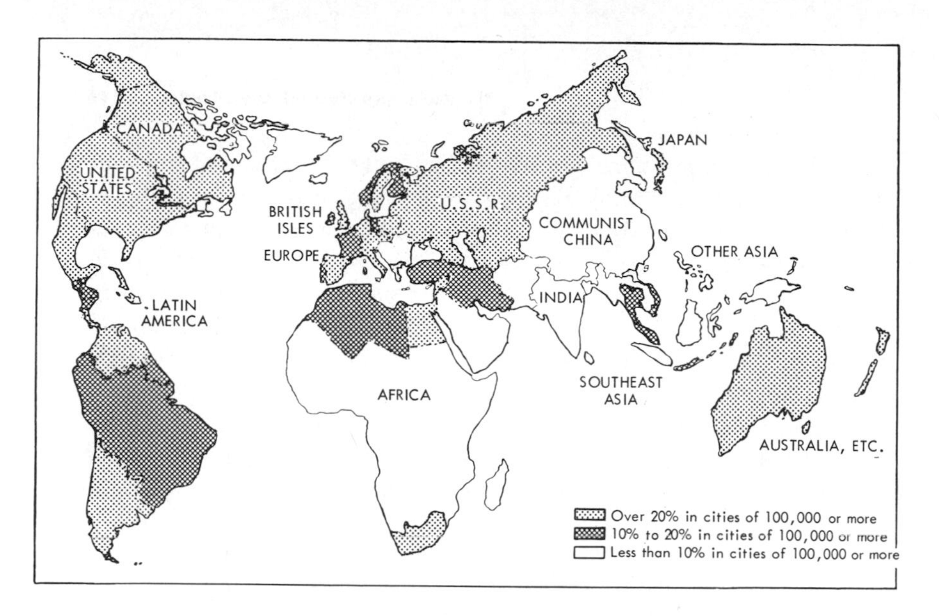

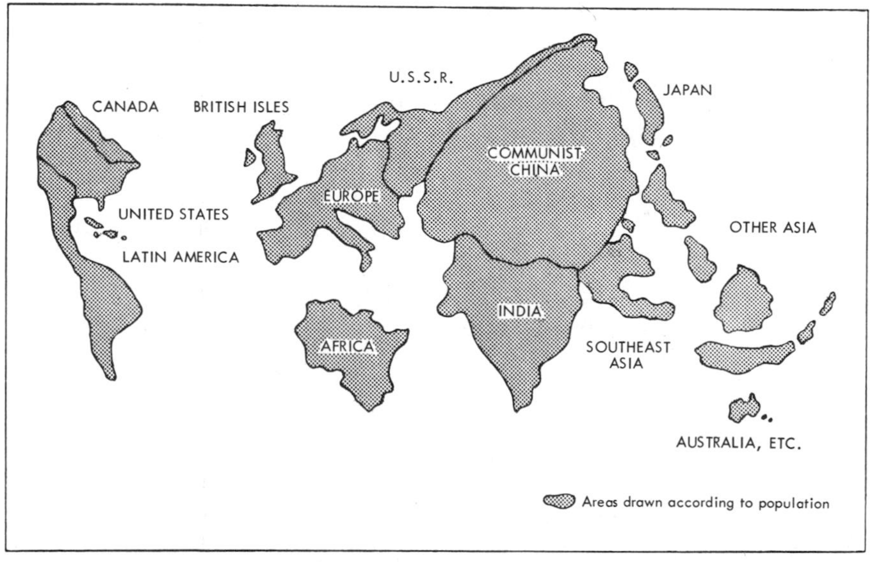

FIGURE 2

Degrees of Urbanization in Major World Regions Compared with World Distribution of Total Population, 1960

Upper map indicates that highly urbanized countries are concentrated in North America and Europe. Lower map, showing areas of the world drawn to scale according to total population in 1960, indicates why the study of cities must include those in non-Western, less-urbanized areas. Many of the least urbanized countries have enormous populations and, hence, already contain large numbers of urban dwellers.

Source: Noel P. Gist and Sylvia F. Fava, Urban Society, 5th ed. *(New York: Thomas Y. Crowell Company, 1964), p. 64, Fig. 7. Lower map copyright 1962 by The New York Times Company. Reprinted by permission.*

Homer Hoyt, using somewhat different calculations but data similar to the above, indicates that by 1960 the percentage of world population living in cities with populations of 20,000 or more had risen to 27.12 per cent, involving over 803 million persons. Of this 27.12 per cent, 19.92 per cent, or over 590 million, were living in places of 100,000 or more population.[3]

Urbanization on the scale to which Westerners are now accustomed, and which may be anticipated elsewhere in the near future, has not been a common feature of the history of the world. Data on the size of early settlements are difficult to secure, but as far as the Western world is concerned the only major urbanization in cities of any substantial size was around the Mediterranean and in connection with the development of the Roman Empire. Hoyt and other researchers have estimated[4] that at the period of greatest development of the Roman Empire, perhaps around A.D. 150, in the total population of the Empire there may have been some 10 million people living in cities of substantial size. Hoyt[5] indicates that Rome may have had a population of 1,000,000, Alexandria 750,000, Seleucia 600,000, Antioch and Carthage each 250,000, plus a half dozen or so cities of over 100,000 population in Asia Minor. However, with the decline of the Roman Empire the population of these cities was greatly reduced. It has been estimated, for example, that, at the time of Augustus, Rome had a population of 1,000,000; this had dropped to 17,000 by the ninth century. There was subsequently a long interval between the decline of the Roman Empire and the development of industrialization in the nineteenth century.

WORLD URBANIZATION SINCE 1800

It was not until the nineteenth century that there was a potential for the development of cities of any size, partly due to increases in agricultural surplus, improved transportation, and political security. Once urbanization began it proceeded apace, as suggested by Table 1 and Figure 3, which show the percentage of increase in total population and world urban population in the 50-year periods 1800–1850, 1850–1900, and 1900–1950.

The emerging pattern is almost unbelievable. While the percentage of increase in total world population was advancing from 29 per cent in the 1800–1850 period to as high as 49 per cent in 1900–1950, the per-

[3] Homer Hoyt, *World Urbanization: Expanding Population in a Shrinking World* (Washington, D.C.: Urban Land Institute, 1962), p. 31, Table 3.
[4] *Ibid.*, p. 8.
[5] *Ibid.*

Table 1
Per Cent of Increase in Total World Population and in World Urban Population: 1800–1850, 1850–1900, 1900–1950 *

Years	Total world population % increase	World population living in agglomerations of 20,000 inhabitants or more % increase	World population living in agglomerations of 100,000 inhabitants or more % increase
1800–1850	29.2	132.3	76.3
1850–1900	37.3	193.5	222.2
1900–1950	49.3	239.6	254.1

* *Source:* United Nations Secretariat, Bureau of Social Affairs, in cooperation with International Labor Office, Food and Agriculture Organization, United Nations Educational, Scientific and Cultural Organization, and World Health Organization, *Report on the World Social Situation Including Studies of Urbanization in Underdeveloped Areas* (New York: United Nations, 1957), p. 114, Table 2.

centage of world population living in places of 20,000 or more increased far more. These cities of 20,000 or more population increased in population as much as 132 per cent in the 1800–1850 period as compared with a total world population increase of 29 per cent; increased 193 per cent in 1850–1900 as compared with a total increase of 37 per cent; and increased 239 per cent in 1900–1950 as compared with a total increase of 49 per cent. At the same time the world population living in great cities —*i.e.*, places of 100,000 or more—showed substantial increases: 76 per cent in the period 1800–1850; 222 per cent in 1850–1900; and 254 per cent in 1900–1950.

The most startling change was in newly developing countries. As the United Nations publication indicates: "Between 1900–1950, the population living in cities of 100,000 or more in Asia mounted from an estimated 19.4 million to 105.6 million (a gain of 444 per cent), and in Africa from 1.4 million to 10.2 million (a gain of 629 per cent)." [6] While the total world population did not even double in the period 1800–1850 as compared with 1900–1950, the percentage of increase in world population living in places of 100,000 or over more than tripled in the same two 50-year periods. The urban revolution was well on its way.

It is particularly significant to note the numerical shifts in urban population that took place between 1800 and 1950, as well as up to

[6] UN, *World Social Situation: 1957*, p. 114.

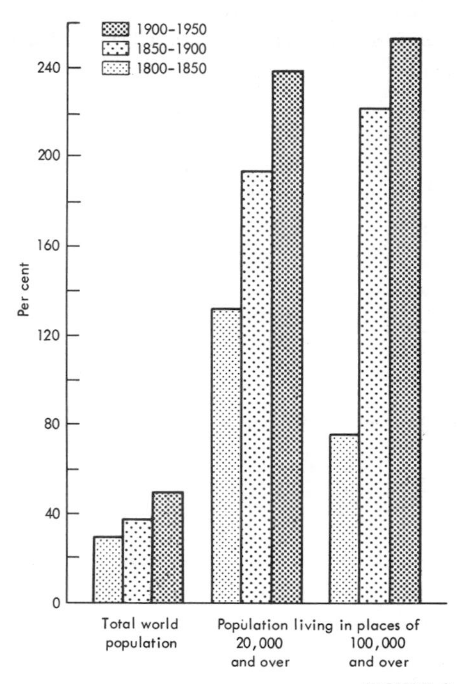

FIGURE 3

The Increase in World and Urban Population

This graph shows the percentage increase in the total population of the world and of the population living in medium-size and large cities since the early part of the Industrial Revolution. During this time, world population increased at a rate unprecedented in previous history, but the movement into cities was far more rapid. In these explosive growing urban areas will be found some of the most serious political, social, and economic problems in the next fifty years. *Source: "The World's Great Cities: Evolution or Devolution?"* Population Bulletin, **16** *(September 1960), 118, Fig. 2.*

1960.[7] As Table 2 shows, while world population increased more than three times in the period 1800–1960, the population living in localities of 20,000 or more inhabitants increased over 40 times. Similarly, the population living in localities of 20,000 to 100,000 inhabitants increased almost 35 times. Concurrently the population living in localities of 100,000 or more increased nearly 40 times. There is clearly no evidence that the world's population increase in urban areas is declining; indeed, today's

[7] Kingsley Davis and Hilda Hertz, "Patterns of World Urbanization," for 1800–1950, as reproduced in UN, *World Social Situation: 1957,* p. 114; 1960 data are based on Homer Hoyt, *op. cit.,* p. 31; data in the 1960 entries are approximately comparable.

Table 2
Total World Population and World Urban Population: 1800–1960 *

	Total world population	Population living in localities of 20,000 inhabitants or more		Population living in localities of 20,000 to 100,000 inhabitants		Population living in localities of 100,000 inhabitants or more	
Year	Millions	Millions	% of world population	Millions	% of world population	Millions	% of world population
1800	906	21.7	2.4	6.1	0.7	15.6	1.7
1850	1,171	50.4	4.3	22.9	2.0	27.5	2.3
1900	1,608	147.9	9.2	59.3	3.7	88.6	5.5
1950	2,400	502.2	20.9	188.5	7.8	313.7	13.1
1960	2,962	803.2	27.1	213.1	7.2	590.0	19.9

* *Source:* Kingsley Davis and Hilda Hertz, "Patterns of World Urbanization for 1800–1950," as reproduced in United Nations Secretariat, Bureau of Social Affairs, in cooperation with the International Labor Office, Food and Agriculture Organization of the United Nations, United Nations Educational, Scientific and Cultural Organization, and World Health Organization, *Report on the World Social Situation Including Studies of Urbanization in Underdeveloped Areas* (New York: United Nations, 1957), p. 114, Table 1. The 1960 data are based on Homer Hoyt, *World Urbanization: Expanding Population in a Shrinking World* (Washington, D.C.: Urban Land Institute, 1962), p. 31, Table 3; data are approximately comparable with those for 1800–1950.

urban way of life for hundreds of millions is vastly different from the predominantly rural pattern of a few short generations ago.

URBANIZATION IN MAJOR GEOGRAPHIC REGIONS

Returning to the 50-year interval presented in Table 1, it is interesting to observe how the distribution of world population by large geographic regions had developed by 1950 (see Table 3). The data in Table 3 should be interpreted with caution, but assuming that the world population is represented as 100 per cent, the table shows the proportion of the 1950 population living in places of 20,000 or more and 100,000 or more as compared with the proportion of the total population living in various geographical areas. It may be surprising to observe that, of all major geographic areas, Asia has the highest percentage of the total world population living both in places of 20,000 and more, and 100,000 and more. It is important to avoid confusion between the percentage of the

Table 3
Distribution of the World Urban Population by Large Geographic Regions: 1950 *

	Distribution of the total world population	Distribution of the world urban population	
		Population living in localities of 20,000 inhabitants and more	Population living in localities of 100,000 inhabitants and more
World	100 %	100 %	100 %
Asia	53.2	33.8	33.7
Europe [a]	16.4	27.5	26.5
North America [b]	6.8	13.9	15.2
U.S.S.R.	8.1	12.0	11.2
South America	4.6	5.8	6.5
Africa	8.2	3.7	3.2
Middle America [c]	2.1	2.1	2.0
Oceania	0.5	1.2	1.6

[a] Except the U.S.S.R.
[b] Including the United States and Canada
[c] Including the countries of Central America, Mexico, and the Caribbean
* *Source:* Kingsley Davis and Hilda Hertz, "Patterns of World Urbanization." Table reproduced in United Nations, *Report on the World Social Situation Including Studies of Urbanization in Underdeveloped Areas,* prepared by the Bureau of Social Affairs, United Nations Secretariat, in cooperation with the International Labor Office, Food and Agriculture Organization of the United Nations, World Health Organization, and the United Nations Educational, Scientific, and Cultural Organization (New York: United Nations, 1957), p. 115, Table 4.

population living in places of 100,000 or more in each *region* of the world (see Table 4) and total *world* population percentages (see Table 3). It is possible for a large percentage of the population of a *region* to be living in cities of a specified size without that region's having a large percentage of the *world* population living in cities of that size.

Because of national differences in definition of *urban* in various parts of the world it has generally been agreed that in comparing urbanization among countries and regions, the word urban will be reserved for places of 20,000 or more inhabitants, and that calculations indicating degrees of urbanization will be based on places of 20,000 or more and places of 100,000 or more population. The underlying assumption here is that it is not until a population of 20,000 is reached that typical characteristics of urban living are likely to appear.

Special interest is always directed to places with populations of

100,000 or more as particularly good indicators of "real" urbanization. (Attention is drawn to the appropriate columns in Tables 1 and 2.) Already noted is the significant difference between the increase in total world population living in places of 100,000 or more in 1800–1850 (76 per cent) and in 1900–1950 (254 per cent). Perhaps even more surprising is the observation that in 1800 only 15.6 million persons were living in places of 100,000 or more, but by 1950 this had increased to 313.7 million persons, and the related percentage of the world population changed accordingly from 1.7 per cent to 13.1 per cent (see Table 2). The change in the *number* of persons living in such large places was much more impressive than the related *percentage* of the total world population change.

There is a wide range in "great city" phenomena in various parts of the world, and many changes have taken place during the last 150 years. Table 4 shows population in cities of 100,000 and over by major continental regions for the years 1800, 1850, 1900, and 1950, together with a supplementary calculation for 1960. Table 4 is self-explanatory, but it should be noted that the columns referring to population in millions can be read vertically, that is, the total for the world is the sum of the various major continental regions. The per cent columns, however, are not additive vertically. The first four sections of the table refer to dates at 50-year intervals, whereas the last section of the table involves a 10-year interval from 1950 to 1960 and comes from a different source, though the data appear to be quite comparable.

In 1800 Asia accounted for nearly two thirds of the world's population in cities of 100,000 or more. Its population declined in 1850 and 1900 but then recovered strongly, so that by 1950 Asia had nearly one third of the total population of the world living in places of 100,000 or more population; by 1960 this proportion was a little less than one third. The twentieth century is quite clearly the period during which urbanization has been proceeding at the greatest rate of increase in newly developing countries of the world.

How do these figures compare with Western experience? In contrast to what had been happening in Asia and Africa, Europe and America had their greatest growth in the nineteenth century, with a considerable decrease thereafter. Two vastly different geographic areas, Oceania and America, in 1960 had about the same *percentage* of their total regional populations living in places of 100,000 or more, although the actual populations were respectively 7 million and 170 million. In the case of Oceania, as high as 21.7 per cent of the total population lived in cities of 100,000 or more as early as 1900. Assuming that the statistics are comparable, it is interesting to compare the 10-year difference between 1950

Table 4

Population in Large Cities (100,000 and Over) by Major Continental Regions: 1800–1960 *

Area	1800		1850		1900		1950		1960	
	In millions	As % of total population in region	In millions	As % of total population in region	In millions	As % of total population in region	In millions	As % of total population in region	In millions	As % of total population in region
World	15.6	1.7	27.5	2.3	88.6	5.5	313.7	13.1	590.0	19.9
Asia	9.8	1.6	12.2	1.7	19.4	2.1	105.6	7.5	203.6	12.3
Europe [a]	5.4	2.9	13.2	4.9	48.0	11.9	118.2	19.9	189.0	29.6
Africa	0.30	0.3	0.25	0.2	1.4	1.1	10.2	5.2	20.4	8.1
America	0.13	0.4	1.8	3.0	18.6	12.8	74.6	22.6	169.9	42.0
Oceania	—	—	—	—	1.3	21.7	5.1	39.2	7.0	43.3

[a] Including the U.S.S.R.

* *Source:* Kingsley Davis and Hilda Hertz, "Patterns of World Urbanization." Table reproduced in United Nations, *Report on the World Social Situation,* including studies of urbanization in underdeveloped areas, prepared by the Bureau of Social Affairs, United Nations Secretariat, in cooperation with the International Labor Office, Food and Agriculture Organization, World Health Organization, and the United Nations Educational, Scientific, and Cultural Organization (New York: United Nations, 1957), p. 114, Table 3. The 1960 data are based on Homer Hoyt, *World Urbanization: Expanding Population in a Shrinking World* (Washington, D.C.: Urban Land Institute, 1962), p. 31, Table 3. Data are approximately comparable with those for 1800–1950.

and 1960 with the 50-year differences in preceding periods. If projected for the future, the percentage increases over the next 10-year period would quite clearly presage a burgeoning urbanization.

Knowing the very large numbers of world population still living in rural areas, it is surprising to imagine that in 1960 one out of every five persons on the surface of the earth lived in a place of 100,000 or more population. In Africa and Asia, of course, the proportions vary greatly from this world average.

These brief observations on the varying degrees of urbanization in the world at different periods inevitably raise the question of projection into the future trend. This subject is discussed in Chapter Five.

ASIAN, AFRICAN, AND LATIN AMERICAN URBAN PATTERNS

Asian Urbanization

We will now turn to a somewhat more detailed examination of the specific pattern of urbanization in Asia, Africa, and Latin America.

The wide variety in sizes and types of countries in Asia produces a complex picture of urbanization.[8] Therefore, generalizations must be made and used with great care, taking particular note of the historical periods, countries, and sub-areas to which they apply.

One of the most enlightening analyses of urbanization in Asia before 1950 has been presented by Jean Chesneaux.[9] J. E. Spencer's summary of this paper calls attention to Chesneaux's major points, including the observation that many Asiatic cities were originally related to the great agricultural empires of the time but have acquired more and more characteristics of Occidental cities as they have developed in recent years. Chesneaux notes that various kinds of civil conflict in such countries as China, India, and the Holy Land led to large numbers of refugees moving into the central cities: "Shanghai's population rose from 4 million to 6

[8] The following publications, selected from many, deal with urbanization in various Asian countries and in Asia as a whole: Philip M. Hauser, ed., *Urbanization in Asia and the Far East,* proceedings of the joint UN/UNESCO seminar, in co-operation with the International Labor Office, *Urbanization in the ECAFE Region,* Bangkok, August 8–18, 1956 (Calcutta: Research Center on the Social Implications of Industrialization in Southern Asia, 1957) (hereafter referred to as UNESCO, *Asia and the Far East*); "Aspects of Urbanization in ECAFE Countries," *Economic Bulletin for Asia and the Far East,* **4**, 1 (Bangkok: United Nations Economic Commission for Asia and the Far East (ECAFE), May 1953).

[9] Jean Chesneaux, "Notes sur l'évolution récente de l'habitat urbaine en Asie," *L'Information Géographique,* **13** (1949), 169–75, and **14** (1950), 1–8. This article is summarized by J. E. Spencer in "Changing Asiatic Cities," *Geographical Review,* **41** (April 1951), 336–37.

million people in a very brief time; that of Karachi from 200,000 to more than a million; Delhi was changed from a large Moslem-Hindu city to a larger Sikh-Hindu city." [10]

Most impressive is the enormous population of the larger countries of the world and the relative differences in proportions of their populations living in urban areas of different sizes about 1960. Considering for a moment the population living in places of one million or more, it is notable that, insofar as data are available, the range in percentage living in such large cities is very great. There is a block of countries with less than 10 per cent of their population in such cities (Pakistan 2.2, China 4.8, India 5.1, Thailand 5.2, Indonesia 6.1, and the Philippines 8.2), and another group with roughly twice these percentages (Turkey 11.6, South Korea 12.0, and South Vietnam 14.3) in this category. Japan, not considered in the same category of newly developing countries as those primarily discussed in this study, had a percentage of 24.5 living in cities of one million or more population. Singapore with 61.2 per cent and Hong Kong with virtually 100 per cent were also in this category. With the exception of Singapore and Hong Kong plus South Vietnam, many of the countries of Asia have cities of one million or more population but also have substantial proportions of their populations living in places of 100,000 or more but less than one million.

One of the great puzzles for countries outside the Soviet bloc is the extent of urbanization in Communist China. As might be expected, there is relatively little information available. Estimates have been made from time to time and one source notes that:

> It has been estimated that 20 million Chinese migrated from rural to urban areas between 1949 and 1956. This almost equals the total population of the three Benelux countries (Belgium, the Netherlands, and Luxembourg) and "undoubtedly constitutes one of history's largest population shifts in so short a time." China's inland cities have experienced fantastic growth. Estimates indicate that in the western provinces alone, Lanchow grew from 200,000 in 1950 to 680,000 in 1956; Paotow from 90,000 in 1949 to 430,000 in 1957;

[10] J. E. Spencer summarizes Chesneaux's materials by referring to the schematic maps Chesneaux prepared of Canton, Bombay, Colombo, Delhi, Bangkok, Haifa, Tehran, Kalgan and Peking: "Of 27 Asiatic cities over a million each in population, nine attained their size in the pre-European period of the great agricultural empires: Cairo, Baghdad, Lahore, Delhi, Canton, Nanking, Peking, Hankow and Kyoto. Seven cities date from the mercantile-colonial era: Madras, Bombay, Calcutta, Karachi, Shanghai, Tientsin, and Hong Kong. Eleven cities achieved their prosperity recently, out of industrialization and a political rejuvenation of the state: Tehran, Bangkok, Chungking, Shihchiachuang, Mukden, Harbin, Yokohama, Tokyo, Osaka, Kobe, and Nagoya."

Kalgan from 270,000 in 1949 to over 630,000 in 1958; Sian from less than one half million in 1949 to 1,050,000 in 1957.[11]

Why these major shifts? Writing in January 1959, Leo A. Orleans discussed in some detail the importance of "push" from collectivization and "pull" from industrialization as factors involved in China's urbanization. He notes that apparently the urbanization which resulted was so great that it became necessary, as a policy matter, to send people from the cities back to their rural areas and to establish other measures to restrict urbanization. Most of these measures, Orleans points out, were ineffectual. The influx to the cities, in the case of China under these circumstances, was referred to as "blind infiltration" of "non-productive elements." Although data are scarce, there is every reason to believe from precedents elsewhere that a substantial amount of urbanization is taking place in Communist China.[12]

Studying world urbanization in terms of the *continental* divisions is not entirely satisfactory. For example, urbanization in southwest Asia might very properly be discussed in connection with Africa, even though it lies outside the African continent; and the Middle East or Near East and the eastern Mediterranean areas are culturally related to the Moslem area of Northern Africa.[13]

Pausing for a moment, then, on the Middle East or Mediterranean countries, we will note that in the eastern Mediterranean parts of what are otherwise classified as Asia, the percentage distribution of population in places of 100,000 or more ranges widely from Jordan (7.3) and Saudi Arabia (8.4) to Turkey (16.2) and Iraq (17.9), with Syria (27.3) and Lebanon (33.2) being the highest in percentage except Israel, a special case at 47.7 per cent. Included in the African portion of the Middle East should be such countries as Egypt (23.7), Algeria (12.7), and Libya (14.5). Published studies dealing with the Middle Eastern- and

[11] "The World's Great Cities: Evolution or Devolution?" *Population Bulletin,* **16** (September 1960), 121–22. See also: Sen-Dou Chang, "The Historical Trend of Chinese Urbanization," *Annals of the Association of American Geographers,* **53** (June 1963), 109–43; Morris B. Ullman, *Cities of Mainland China: 1953–59,* U.S. Bureau of the Census, Foreign Manpower Research Office, International Population Reports, Series P-95, No. 59 (Washington, D.C.: U.S. Government Printing Office, August 1961) (using the best data available at the time), p. 15, Table F.

[12] Leo A. Orleans, "The Recent Growth of China's Urban Population," *Geographical Review,* **49** (January 1959), 43–57.

[13] It has been impossible to secure maps showing the distribution of urban population for all of Asia. However, for one particular segment of Asia, *i.e.,* Southwest Asia, which is sometimes included in the Near or Middle East but for our purposes is classified under Asia, there is a map available, as shown in George B. Cressey, *Crossroads: Land and Life in Southwest Asia* (Philadelphia: J. B. Lippincott Co., 1960), p. 40, Fig. 4.

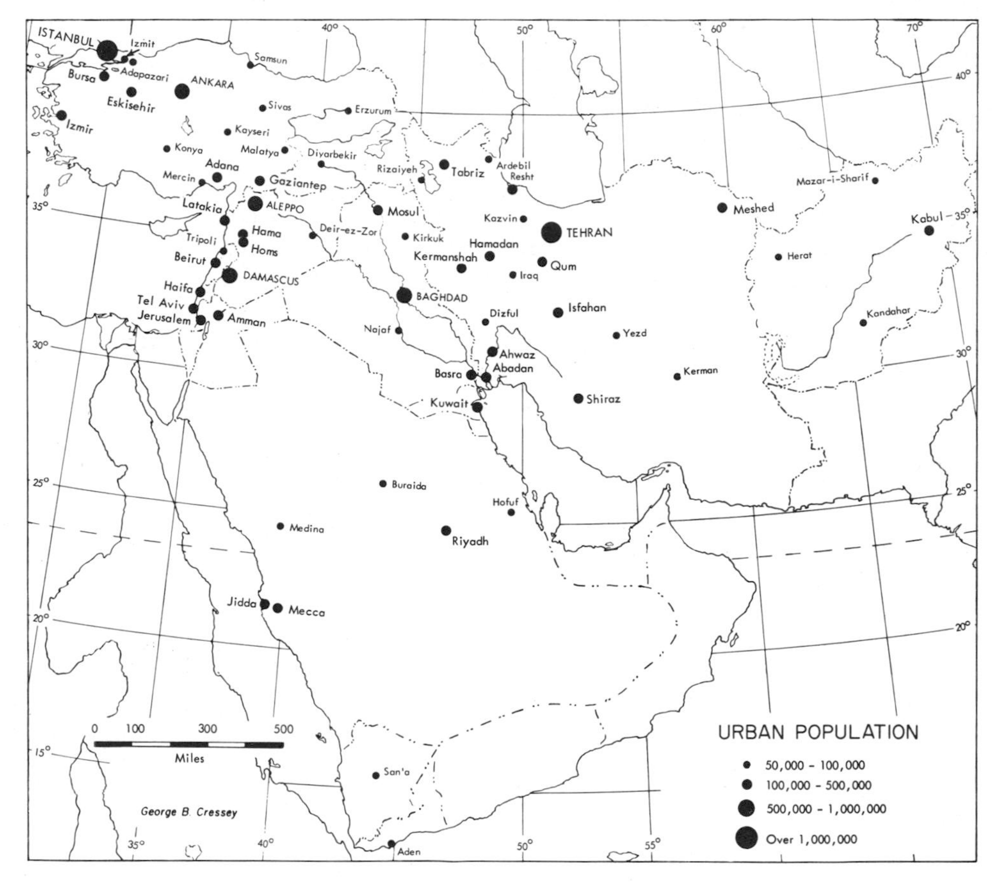

FIGURE 4

Southwest Asia: Urban Centers

Source: George B. Cressey, Crossroads: Land and Life in Southwest Asia *(Philadelphia: J. B. Lippincott Co., 1960), p. 40. Reprinted by permission.*

Moslem-type cities are available, but in general these studies do not provide data useful at this particular point in our discussion.[14]

African Urbanization

The evidence clearly qualifies Africa to be the least urbanized (in terms of population in places of 1,000,000 and more) of all the conti-

[14] An exception is one of the early working monographs prepared under an Air Force contract: Donald L. Foley, Judith Blake, Hilda Hertz, and Suzette Kettler, "The Mediterranean Region and Its Cities" (New York: Columbia University Bureau of Applied Social Research, August 1953).

nents in the world. As a whole Africa is urbanized to this extent less than 10 per cent, and virtually every African country is urbanized less than 10 per cent, with the exception of Egypt and the Republic of South Africa (the latter of which is not considered to be a typical newly developing African country).

Figure 5 shows in schematic form the areas south of the Sahara which

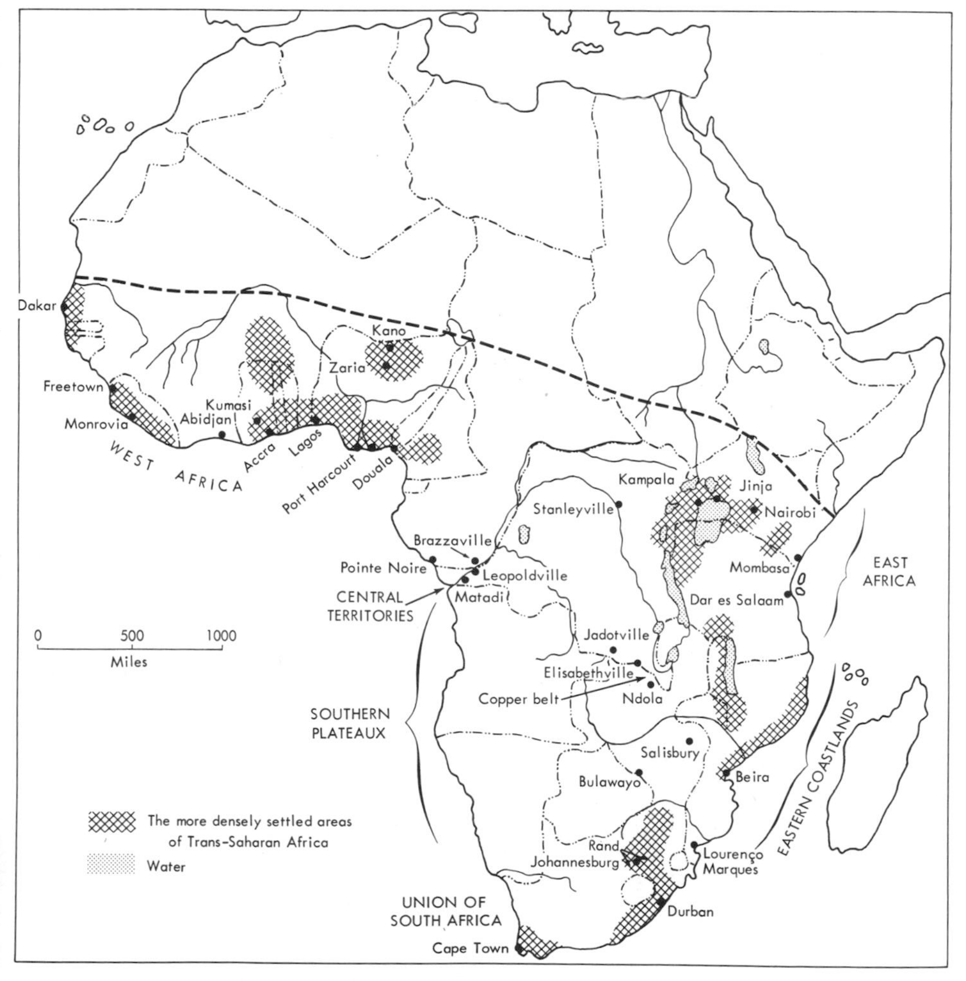

FIGURE 5

Africa: Areas South of the Sahara in Process of Urbanization

Source: The International African Institute, London, Social Implications of Industrialization and Urbanization in Africa South of the Sahara *(Paris: UNESCO, 1956), p. 15. Prepared under the auspices of UNESCO.*

are definable as being in process of urbanization. The primate city phenomenon, discussed in detail in Chapter Two, characterizes most of the West African countries and many others south of the Sahara.

Urbanization in West Africa—or, for that matter, in various other parts of Africa—is difficult to analyze by country. National units reflect the arbitrary drawing of boundaries long ago by Europeans to fit their own particular interests, thus by intention or ignorance dividing established cultural and functional areas. The result is that the urban development of these countries has often had to take place within, or in spite of, unusual constraints.

With one notable exception discussed briefly below, urbanization in West Africa in particular is confined almost entirely to coastal areas. If the rate of urbanization in western and middle African countries were measured in terms of growth of these larger coastal cities only, the rates would be very high but they would not be representative of their total national populations.

The very early urbanization—albeit of a somewhat different sort from that of modern times—among the Yoruba, in what is presently Nigeria, merits special mention. The Yoruba lived in cities of substantial size even before Europeans arrived on this part of the African continent.[15] As early as 1856 there were nine Yoruban cities of over 20,000, including three of over 60,000 population. By 1911 the number of Yoruban "cities" had increased to eleven, with five having over 60,000 population; by 1952 there were nine such cities. The dominance of the Yoruban urban complex in West Africa may be clearly seen in Figure 6, which shows the distribution of urban population in tropical Africa.

As William Bascom points out, not only was there extensive urbanization among the Yoruba at a fairly early period, but the density of population involved was very high:

> Population densities of 87,000 per square mile for Lagos in 1950; 55,555 for Ibadan in 1960; and 43,372 for Ogbomosho, 13,914 for Oyo, and 5,720 for Abeokuta in 1931, compare with 24,697 for New York City, 15,850 for Chicago, 15,743 for Philadelphia, and 5,451 for Los Angeles—the four largest urban centers in the United States—in 1960.[16]

[15] A. L. Mabogunje, *Yoruba Towns* (Ibadan, Nigeria: Ibadan University Press, 1962), p. 1. See also: N. C. Mitchel, "Yoruba Towns," in K. M. Barbour and R. M. Prothero, eds., *Essays in African Population* (New York: Frederick A. Praeger, Inc., 1962), pp. 279–301; G. Hamdan, "Capitals of the New Africa," *Economic Geography,* **40,** 3 (July 1964), 239–53.

[16] William Bascom, "Some Aspects of Yoruba Urbanism," *American Anthropologist,* **64** (August 1962), 699.

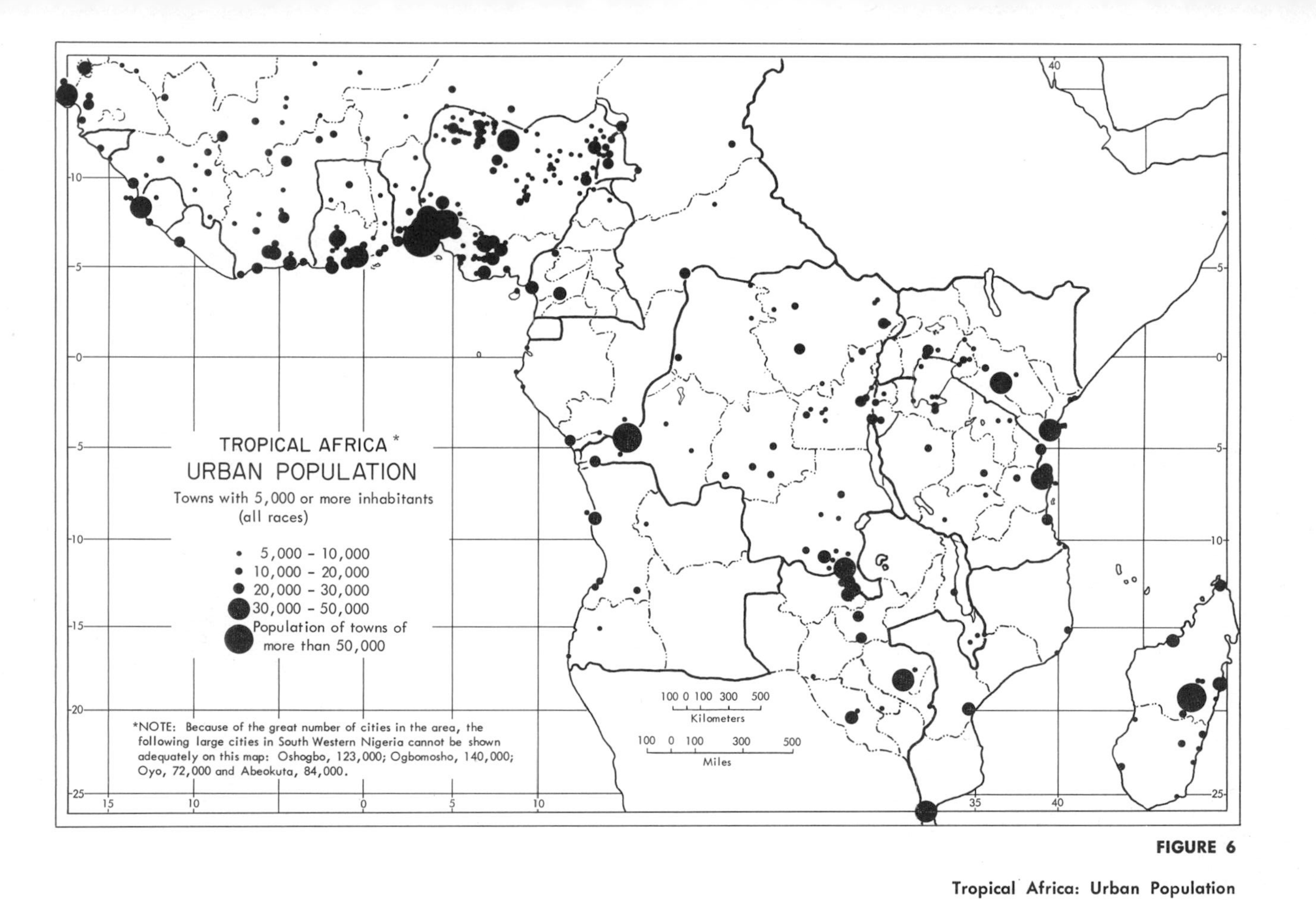

FIGURE 6

Tropical Africa: Urban Population

Source: A. L. Mabogunje, Yoruba Towns *(Ibadan, Nigeria: Ibadan University Press, 1962), Fig. 1.*

Virtually all African cities, no matter what their size, and particularly those with over 100,000 population, are attempting to cope with substantial migration into their metropolitan areas as a result of the World War II shifts in population and subsequent international conflicts. In 1964, for example, it was reported that in Burundi there were 80,000 homeless refugees, in the Congo about 40,000, and in Uganda some 100,000.[17]

Latin and South American Urbanization

Urbanization in Latin and South America exhibits some major differences from that in other newly developing areas. In Latin America, or at least in that North American portion of it south of the Rio Grande, somewhat the same kinds of problems are encountered as in the case of the continental disposition of the Middle East with reference to Africa and Asia. The urbanization taking place south of the Rio Grande in North America has much more in common with that of South America than with the United States and Canada.[18] In many respects this area more properly belongs with South America and will be so considered here.

In only one South American country (Bolivia) is the percentage of the population living in cities of 100,000 or more less than about 15 per cent, with a number of the countries having about 30 to 35 per cent and Argentina having 52.2 per cent in this category. On the other hand, in Latin America—*i.e.*, islands between North and South America, and

[17] "Refugee Problem Besets Africans," *The New York Times,* March 1, 1965 (article dated Nairobi, Kenya, February 28, 1965). See also: Hilda Kuper, ed., *Urbanization and Migration in West Africa* (Berkeley, Calif.: University of California Press, 1965); Kenneth L. Little, ed., "Special Number on Urbanism in West Africa," *Sociological Review,* 7 (July 1959), 3–122; and for references to urbanism in Africa prior to 1950, see Jean L. Comhaire (compiler), *Urban Conditions in Africa: Select Reading List on Urban Problems in Africa* (London: Geoffrey Cumberlege, Oxford University Press for Institute of Colonial Studies, 1950) (a revision of an earlier edition published in May 1947). *Cf.* Ruth P. Simms, *Urbanization in West Africa: A Review of Current Literature* (Evanston, Illinois: Northwestern University Press, 1965).

[18] Among the most useful sources of data on the extent of urbanization in South and Latin America are such publications as the following: Philip M. Hauser, ed., *Urbanization in Latin America* (Paris: UNESCO, 1961); Homer Hoyt, "The Residential and Retail Patterns of Leading Latin American Cities," *Land Economics,* **39,** 4 (November 1963), 449–54; Kingsley Davis, "Colonial Expansion and Urban Diffusion in the Americas," *International Journal of Comparative Sociology,* **1** (March 1960), 43–66; Harley L. Browning, "Recent Trends in Latin American Urbanization," *Annals of the American Academy of Political and Social Science,* **316** (March 1958), 111–20; Louis E. Guzman, *An Annotated Bibliography of Publications on Urban Latin America* (Chicago: University of Chicago Press, Department of Geography, 1952); and Albert G. H. Dietz, Marcia N. Koth, and Julia A. Silvo, *Housing in Latin America* (Cambridge, Mass.: Massachusetts Institute of Technology Press, 1965), esp. pp. 1–28.

North America south of the Rio Grande—the smaller countries have a very small percentage (less than 10 per cent) living in cities of over 100,000 population (Costa Rica, El Salvador, Haiti, and Honduras). Several countries have cities in population categories of 100,000 or over within the range of 23 to 31 per cent (Jamaica, Panama, Cuba, Mexico, and Puerto Rico). It is notable that percentages living in places with populations of one million or over are reported for the following countries: Colombia 8.0, Mexico 10.7, Cuba 18.1, Brazil 12.7, Peru 11.6, Chile 22.3, and Venezuela 20.2—all data as of approximately 1960. It will also be noted, for comparative purposes, that in all of South America the average percentage living in places of 100,000 or over population is 27.4, and the average percentage living in places of one million or over for all of South America is 14.7. Five countries in particular have relatively high ratings for percentage of urbanization: Argentina, Chile, Uruguay, Cuba, and Venezuela.[19] A brief summary of the major demographic aspects of urbanization in Latin America is presented in a UNESCO study.[20] During its rapid urbanization, Latin America—as well as North America and Australia—bypassed "the slow evolution from densely settled peasant-agrarianism to modern industrialization." [21]

URBANIZATION BY COUNTRY: PER CENT URBAN AND SIZE OF PLACES

Table 5 provides a summary of the number of cities by selected size classes and by major geographic area. This is, in effect, a frequency count of the number of cities of two major size categories in each area according to the latest available information. Wide variations in the number of cities of different sizes are readily observable. The detailed data from which this table was prepared include instances of countries which have, in effect, only one large urban area, the primate city situation to which reference will be made later, and those that have dozens or even hundreds of cities of various sizes, indicating a much more intensive and extensive level of urbanization.[22]

[19] See also UNESCO, *Latin America,* p. 27.

[20] UNESCO, *Latin America,* pp. 91–93. See also Carmen A. Miro, "The Population of Latin America," *Demography,* 1 (1964), 15–41, esp. Tables 5–9.

[21] Kingsley Davis and Hilda Hertz Golden, "Urbanization and the Development of Pre-Industrial Areas," *Economic Development and Cultural Change,* 3 (October 1954), 9.

[22] For persons wishing more detail and more refined and multiple breakdowns of places by size group, reference should be made to the sources used in construction of this table: *UN Demographic Yearbooks* for 1960, 1962, and 1963, Tables 8, 11, and 32 respectively.

Table 5

Number of Places by Size Class in Selected Major Geographic Areas, ca. 1960 *

Continent	Number of Places: 100,000 and over	20,000 and over
Africa	62	405
North America [a]	36	248
South America	82	436
Asia [b]	431	2291
Oceania [c]	12	40

Data for all continents includes some for places 25,000 and over instead of 20,000 and over.

[a] Does *not* include the United States, Canal Zone (U.S.), or the Virgin Islands

[b] Does *not* include the Maldive Islands

[c] Does *not* include American Samoa, the Cook Islands, the Fiji Islands, Gilbert and Ellice Islands, Guam, or Western Samoa

* *Sources:* United Nations Department of Economic and Social Affairs, *Demographic Yearbook 1960* (New York: United Nations, 1960), pp. 349–71, Table 8; United Nations Department of Economic and Social Affairs, *Demographic Yearbook 1962* (New York: United Nations, 1962), pp. 380–96, Table 11; United Nations Department of Economic and Social Affairs, *Demographic Yearbook 1963* (New York: United Nations, 1964), pp. 696–703, Table 32 (supplement to Table 11 in *Demographic Yearbook 1962*).

United Nations data [23] conveniently summarize changes in places of 20,000 and over population from 1950 to 1960, in "less" and "more" developed regions. Table 6 shows the 1950 and 1960 regional estimated per cent distributions of world total and urban populations, and percentages of population in places of 20,000 or more. The table is self-explanatory.

Table 7 is a concise listing of countries having differing levels of urbanization in 1960—the current level of urbanization for particular newly developing countries as compared with other countries.

CONCLUSION

The characteristics of urbanization in newly developing countries are best understood in the context of the total changes in each growing country. Differences in urbanization may arise because the urbanization has taken place in the periods of colonization or exploitation by foreign countries, or in connection with the emergence of nationhood following

[23] United Nations Economic and Social Council, "World Survey of Urban and Rural Population Growth: Preliminary Report by the Secretary-General," E/CN.9/187 (March 8, 1965), for Population Commission, 13th sess., Item 4 of the provisional agenda (24 pp. processed), Tables 3 and 4.

Table 6

Estimated Per Cent Distribution of World Population, and Percentages of Population in Places of 20,000 or More Inhabitants for the Regions of the World, 1950–1960

Area	Estimated % distribution of world population		% of population in places of 20,000 or more: Estimated averages for all countries			% of population in places of 20,000 or more: Averages for countries having 1950 and 1960 data		
	1950	1960	1950	1960	% increase in proportion urban [a]	1950	1960	% increase in proportion urban [a]
World Total	100	100	21	24–25[b]	12–17[b]	27	30	12
Less Developed Regions	70	72	14	17–18[b]	17–28[b]	18	22	19
Africa	9	9	10	13	37	14	18	27
North Africa	—	—	21	26	23	25	31	23
Sub-Sahara Africa	—	—	6	9	50	8	11	35
Asia	55	56	14	16–18[b]	11–26[b]	19	21	14
Excluding China (mainland)	33	34	17	19	15	19	21	14
China (mainland)	22	22	10	10–15[b]	0–50[b]	—	—	—
Latin America	6	7	25	32	28	28	36	29
Argentina, Chile, Uruguay	—	—	47	56	19	48	57	20
Remainder of Latin America	—	—	21	28	33	21	29	40
More Developed Regions	30	28	37	41	10	38	41	10
Northern America	7	7	43	46	6	43	46	6
Europe (excluding U.S.S.R.)	16	14	37	40	8	37	40	8
Northwestern	—	—	52	54	3	52	54	3
Central	—	—	37	40	9	37	40	9
Southern	—	—	23	27	16	23	27	16
U.S.S.R.	7	7	31	36	17	31	36	17
Oceania	[c]	[c]	46	53	15	56	64	13
Australia and New Zealand	—	—	58	65	12	58	65	12
Remainder of Oceania	—	—	—	3	—	—	15	—

[a] From unrounded data. [b] Range of estimated values corresponding to alternative estimates for China (mainland). [c] Less than 1%.

Table 7

Classification of Countries According to Level of Urbanization Around 1960 (or Most Recent Census Date) *

	Low: Under 20.0 % of total population in places of 20,000 or more inhabitants	Medium Low: 20.0–29.9 % of total population in places of 20,000 or more inhabitants	Medium High: 30.0–39.9 % of total population in places of 20,000 or more inhabitants	High: 40.0 % or more of total population in places of 20,000 or more inhabitants
Africa				
North Africa	Sudan	Algeria Libya Morocco Tunisia	UAR: Egypt	
South, West, and East Africa	Basutoland Burundi Republic of Cameroun Central African Republic Chad Republic Republic of Congo (Leopoldville) Dahomey Republic Gabon Republic Gambia Ghana Kenya Liberia Malagasy Republic [a] Malawi Mozambique Niger Republic [a] South-West Africa Southern Rhodesia Tanzania and Pemba [a] Republic of Togo Uganda Republic of Upper Volta Zambia	Senegal Republic	Union of South Africa	
North America				Canada United States

Table 7

Classification of Countries According to Level of Urbanization Around 1960 (or Most Recent Census Date) * (Cont.)

	Low: Under 20.0 % of total population in places of 20,000 or more inhabitants	Medium Low: 20.0—29.9 % of total population in places of 20,000 or more inhabitants	Medium High: 30.0—39.9 % of total population in places of 20,000 or more inhabitants	High: 40.0 % or more of total population in places of 20,000 or more inhabitants
Latin America	Costa Rica Dominican Republic El Salvador Guatemala Haiti Honduras	Jamaica Nicaragua Puerto Rico Brazil Colombia (1951) Ecuador Peru	Cuba (1953) Mexico Panama	Argentina Chile Venezuela Uruguay
Asia	Ceylon (1953) India Sabah Sarawak (Malaysia) Pakistan	Cyprus Iran Malasia [a] Turkey	Jordan Ryukyu Islands	Israel Japan
Europe				
Northwestern		Finland	Ireland Luxembourg Norway Northern Ireland	Belgium Denmark France Netherlands Sweden England and Wales Scotland
Central Europe		Czechoslovakia	Austria Hungary Poland Switzerland	East Germany Federal Republic of Germany
Southern Europe	Albania Malta and Gozo Portugal Yugoslavia	Bulgaria Romania	Greece Italy Spain	
Oceania	Fiji			Australia New Zealand
U.S.S.R.			U.S.S.R.	

[a] Name updated since 1960

* *Source:* United Nations Economic and Social Council, "World Survey of Urban and Rural Population Growth: Preliminary Report by the Secretary-General," E/CN.9/187 (March 8, 1965), for Population Commission, 13th sess., Item 4 of the provisional agenda (24 pp. processed), p. 24, Table 5.

the end of colonial experience. It is also important to recognize that, as in the case of the Yoruba in West Africa, there may have been urbanization of considerable magnitude even prior to the colonial period.

Many cities are the result of externally oriented economic development, not indigenous forces. However, there may have been, and may continue to be, factors which substantially affect not only the existing but also the potential rate of urbanization.

Urbanization in newly developing countries was affected by forces outside these countries, as was dramatically illustrated by the impact of World War I and, particularly, World War II. The urbanization of certain countries involved in World War II almost invariably reveals evidence of the conflicts which led to floods of refugees moving toward the large cities, and of the relationship of military staging and supply centers to the development of the cities themselves. The related impetus to manufacturing, commerce, and administrative development associated with the war was also influential. As Jean Chesneaux has pointed out:

> Without doubt, one of the most lasting consequences of the Second World War, in the field of human geography, will be the decisive increase in the role of the great cities. Development of the functional equipment of the state, augmentation of industrial production, enlargement of suburbs, the frequently considerable numerical increase of the urban population, the housing crisis—all these phenomena are world-wide phenomena.[24]

Attention has been called not only to the extent and magnitude of urbanization in newly developing countries but also to the percentage of population involved, variations from place to place, and ranges in the urbanization process.

It is not feasible to relate the degree of urbanization of a country to its overall density of population.[25] It is quite possible to have a relatively high level of urbanization and still have a low density of population for the country as a whole, as in the case of Argentina. The obverse—a relatively high density of population in the country as a whole but a relatively low degree of urbanization—is also possible, as in India. However, the relationship between degree of national urbanization and energy consumption[26] appears to be a useful index: the countries most urbanized are generally those with high energy consumption rates.

[24] Jean Chesneaux, *L'Information Géographique.*

[25] UN, *World Social Situation,* p. 117.

[26] See, for example, Leo F. Schnore, "The Statistical Measurement of Urbanization and Economic Development," *Land Economics,* 37 (August 1961), 229–45. *Cf.* William F. Cottrell, *Energy and Society: The Relation between Energy, Social Change, and Economic Development* (New York: McGraw-Hill Book Company, 1955).

When dealing with a complicated phenomenon such as urbanization, particularly in undertaking a comparison among countries as diverse in their characteristics as those discussed here, comparisons may be very misleading. For example, a city of 100,000 is quite different in its importance in Europe or America as compared with a city of the same size in West Africa or India. The difference is likely to be even more pronounced in the case of cities of one million or more population, particularly in countries having only one such city, the primate city case. The difference in importance may depend upon the size of the country, the total population which is served by the cities, the geographical context—*i.e.*, whether there is another city of similar size nearby—and the kind of city—*i.e.*, the types of functions it performs.

Many questions naturally arise after we examine such data. Why have these enormous increases in urbanization taken place? Why have these increases been so pronounced in the newly developing countries? Why is the urbanization of these countries beginning to assume more and more the characteristics of many of their Western counterparts? Succeeding chapters answer questions such as these.

Urbanization seems invariably to accompany the development of new countries. Why does this happen? Understanding this phenomenon is facilitated by familiarity with both long-term and recent circumstances surrounding the appearance of the cities, and knowledge of the survival and growth factors with which they are associated.

HISTORIC ROLES OF CITIES PRIOR TO MODERNIZATION

Market

Urban centers in West Africa serve as particularly helpful illustrations of the historic roles of cities because of the existence, for a long period of time, of a considerable degree of "urbanization" among the Yoruba in what is now Nigeria.[1] Yoruban urbanization was referred to in Chapter One and will not be enlarged upon here. However, it is of interest that some of the Yoruban cities have survived to the present time as important centers of urbanization in the newly developing countries of which

[1] See William Bascom, "Some Aspects of Yoruban Urbanism," *American Anthropologist*, **64** (August 1962), 699–709, esp. the refs. cited (pp. 108–9) including articles by Bascom in *American Journal of Sociology*, **60** (March 1955), 446–54; *Man*, **58** (1958), 253; *The Sociological Review*, **7** (1959), 29–43, and others. See also A. L. Mabogunje, *Yoruba Towns* (Ibadan, Nigeria: Ibadan University Press, 1962).

CHAPTER TWO

The City: Its Role, Form, and Structure

they became a part.[2] With the exception of this old special type of urbanization, West Africa in general had shown very little evidence of agglomerations of people above the village size prior to contact with traders and colonial interests. There had been some coastal transportation from point to point within West Africa by sea, but it was only with the beginning of trading with the outside world in connection with the slave trade and the small goods trade that cities began to be "necessary" in the West African situation. On the other hand there is considerable history of settlements for some cities, or what later became the cores of cities at crossroads, watering places, and shrines.

Colonial Administrative Center

With the carving up or delimitation of the West African area into spheres of influence by strong European powers, it became necessary to establish small settlements as centers of administration for trade and colonial development. Wherever village or town life had pre-existed, there was an inevitable enlargement of the settlement, in part to provide foodstuffs and services for the new settlers, whether temporary or permanent, and in part to provide headquarters and organization for the collection of goods from the interior and the distribution of whatever materials were taken in trade for the products exported.

During the earlier periods of independence from influences outside the local area, trading was scarce and the necessary goods to be exchanged were relatively small in number and variety. With the emergence of interdependence, however, it became necessary to set up market facilities and to establish or develop functionaries to act as agents of exchange and recorders of agreements between foreigners and native populations.

The gradual increase in the population of the native areas made available a surplus of population which followed the natural course of events in such cases: migration to villages, towns, and cities wherever they existed, often involving considerable sacrifice and inconvenience. Some of the population that went first to the large cities in these countries remained there, some were exported as slaves, and others found it desirable to move up and down the coast to other locations.

As a city grows, its dependence on an agricultural surplus becomes tighter and more crucial, necessitating a certain amount of exchange. There develops an increasing use of money or other symbols of value as substitutes for goods when the value of the product exchanged exceeds the mere needs of the participants themselves. Eventually the rural in-

[2] See Mabogunje, *op. cit.*, Chap. I, *supra*, p. 1, Table 15.

habitants nearby tend to become more and more dependent on the city by providing what the city needs, and some of their wants must therefore be met by a cash nexus.

If the new trade and colonial interests prosper, the probability is that urbanization will increase. There appears to be a correlation between the degree of urbanization and the emergence of self-governing countries.[3] As time passes, the importance of the original location of the trading and colonial enterprises causes the city to emerge as a specialized market for the products.

With the colonial and foreign trading phase at an end, or at least replaced by the emergence of the new self-governing nation, the urban area which tends to be the center continues its function as a market *extraordinaire* and, in addition, performs other functions for the newly emerging country.

URBAN ROLES FOR EMERGING NATIONS

Point of Contact with the "Outside" World

The city tends to become the new country's major point of contact with the "outside" world. The new nation attracts political representatives from other countries and, eventually, travelers and tradesmen who are interested in coming in contact with the new country and its officials. Correspondingly, the city that stands at the head of the emerging country plays a very important role in providing a proper image of the new country to the outsider. This sometimes encourages new countries to erect imposing public structures for prestige purposes as well as for symbols of the new government to the native population.

Locus of Power

The city also becomes extremely important as the major locus of power in the new country. This power is not just that represented by the national government headquarters, which are invariably located in an urban context. In the city are established the policies and programs that determine the dominance or influence this urban political organization is likely to have over the remainder of the country.

The city also becomes the locus of economic power. This derives partly from the fact that it tends to become the headquarters of industrial, commercial, and other enterprises developing within the country or having contacts with countries outside. Supporting this locus of power

[3] See Lyle W. Shannon, "Demographic Characteristics of Non-Self-governing Areas," *Planning Outlook,* **5,** No. 3 (1961), 44.

is the expenditure pattern of the national government, which tends—whether or not by plan—to be concentrated rather intensively in the national capital first among the various cities, if there is more than one major city. The ramifications of this focusing of economic power in the major city of a newly developing country are related to certain factors of inertia. For economic and other reasons once a headquarters is established in a particular city it is unlikely that it will move elsewhere unless—and this happens rarely—the national capital is relocated, as is now in process, for example, in Pakistan and a few other countries. The implications of this centering in a particular city for a city's dominance over the remainder of the country are indeed significant. Once this locus has been established an "all-roads-lead-to-Rome" orientation will rapidly tend to develop.

Agency and Diffusion Point of Social Change

Another significance of the city in newly developing countries is that it serves as the primary agency and diffusion point of social change for the new nation. It is likely that here new ideas of national policy will emerge, new leaders will be discovered, new national programs will be evolved, and the administrative centers for the diffusion, propagation, and implementation of the programs will be centered. It is from here that the bureaucracy—at least until it develops to the point where it can establish effective branch offices—is likely to exercise supreme extensive and intensive control over the life of the city and, correspondingly, of the countryside and thus of the nation.

Receptacle of Talent and Manpower

The capital or primate city early becomes the receptacle of the nation's highest talent as well as its most needy, the new nation's manpower, and its major investment funds. It has not yet been conclusively demonstrated that the city has a differential effect in sorting out and attracting to it only the best in the population. However, there seems to be a coincidence of probability of competent individuals tending to move toward the urban areas. The danger is that the central city or cities may progressively absorb, with little capacity to recirculate, the country's best talents. These persons, having once lived in the city, tend not to be inclined voluntarily or involuntarily to return to the countryside. Quite clearly this represents a real and significant net loss of rural and village leadership. This is typical of urbanization everywhere; the same process appears to be taking place in the cityward migration of rural populations in virtually all Western as well as newly developing countries.

A differential attraction of high talent from villages and agricultural sections to urban areas can create a considerable impact upon the affected rural areas. This attraction may even have rather significant national administrative implications as, for example, does the draining of persons from rural and village areas who might otherwise become representatives of decentralized government programs. Thus there may be a dyseconomy or dysfunction involved in the tendency of high-talent persons to leave villages where it is so necessary to have as many as possible return to these villages for administration of national programs.

Obviously many others than those of highest talent are included among the migrants to urban areas. Since the percentage of exceptional talent in any population is relatively low, it should be expected that the vast majority of migrants to urban areas would not have the same characteristics as leaders or potential leaders may have. As will be pointed out in Chapter Three, this vast majority of the population includes many persons who are most in need, most expendable from agricultural production, and have less leadership experience and potential and, therefore, are more likely to be readily led. The kinds of public mass appeals which can successfully be undertaken by leaders in the national capitals may reflect the relatively unsophisticated character of the great bulk of migrants to urban areas.

Between those migrants who are highly talented and those who are most in need are other persons who, given appropriate opportunities, eventually become the specialists, clerks, tradesmen, and operators of business, as well as the great majority of middle-range participants in the governmental and administrative process.

Place of Investment

Equally important is the fact that the city—or cities—becomes a receptacle for the major investment funds available internally to the country and from outside via foreign aid and industrial and commercial enterprises. The crucial question here is whether this precludes, or may be likely to preclude, the distribution of these national investment funds over the countryside as a whole. In a country that has only one or a primate type of city, the answer assumes great importance since the newly developing country is not likely to have unlimited resources.

Much of what has been discussed above in connection with the developing role of urban areas in the countries with which we are concerned has become evident over a long period of time, and development of different aspects has proceeded at different rates. This development has been held in check under some circumstances either by controls of colonial powers or, subsequently, by controls introduced by new national governments. In other cases, some of the aspects of development have been accelerated through time by the same sources of authority; some have been left to work out their own fates irrespective of much colonial or national intervention. From an examination of a number of these cities in newly developing countries, however, it would appear that a relatively uniform sequence of events—or at least a relatively uniform result—can be observed leading from the processes to which we have referred.

CONTEMPORARY ROLES OF URBAN AREAS

Continuing Functions

Urban areas have three major characteristics resulting from what has happened in these urban areas over a long period. In the first place, the city has had to be responsible for retaining and improving its earlier colonial functions. In addition, it has had to face the responsibilities of a considerable extension of its work and its role. For example, the coming of nationhood has inevitably required the creation of new administrative units and the reorganization of business and industry, not to mention political matters. Personnel and practices have had to be developed for controls over communications, police, new national armies, and similar extensions of administration by the new country.

Center for Domestic and Foreign Activities

A second role of primate cities at present, and likely for some time into the future, is as the locus of commercial, foreign, and international activities. We are not suggesting that if foreign or national investment takes place in certain rural types of activities, such as rubber plantations or various kinds of mining operations, there will not be major administrative units located outside the central city. On the other hand it still is true that, at the minimum, a small office for administrative purposes and maintaining contact with the national government is likely to be retained in the national capital.

Magnet for Rural Population

A third existing function or role of urban centers in newly developing countries is as magnets for the national population, so much so as to induce migration in numbers generally far above the capacity of the city to employ, house, feed, service, and educate. Nevertheless, there continues to be a kind of undiminishable "tropism" affecting the population of newly developing countries, the net result being the undiminished swelling of urban population.

Policy Implications

Not all of the implications of these urban roles can be considered here, but some attention will be directed to four.

The first policy implication should be obvious, and yet it is sometimes only reluctantly admitted even by those who are most in a position to understand why it should be taken into account. We refer to the crucial importance—indeed, necessity—of an urban locus for carrying forward those activities that are indispensable to nationhood in modern times. Administrators and politicians of newly developing countries rather wistfully wish that they did not have to cope with the problems of such urban areas in addition to all the other problems which confront them, for there is no question that urbanization is an extremely important component. Yet these same persons readily admit that no modern nation can hope to exist without at least one urban area. The reasons are apparent and have been suggested in the lists of factors to be taken into account in assessing the role of urban areas in newly developing countries.

The second major policy implication of urbanization concerns the enormous pressure for differential investment of national funds into urban areas. In the case of countries having only one such city, this results in pressure to make the heaviest investments there; where there are more cities, the allocation problem is much more complex.

Because of the exigencies of other responsibilities faced by new nations, there is a tendency to "live with" what appear to be inevitable differentials in allocation of funds favoring cities. The urgent requirements of national defense, organizing new agencies of government, maintaining a level of living tolerable to the new country's population, providing increased educational opportunities and, above all, providing employment, are so great and so complex that it cannot be expected or hoped that much attention will be given to the question of exactly *where* the solutions to problems will be applied. It is obviously much easier to apply any solutions available in the area closest at hand, namely, the urban area.

The third major policy implication of urbanization is one which inevitably follows from an influx of population to urban areas, and the recurrent and inevitable problems that arise in this connection. This is the policy question of how to cope with *short-term* urban problems. As we have noted elsewhere, the numbers of these problems is great and their dimensions are not to be underestimated. An illustration worth noting is the provision of housing and related facilities for the new and swelling population. The problem is universal; its dimensions are almost unmeasurable; its ramifications for the development of the urban population are inestimable. For example, the possible political repercussions of shortcomings in the provision of housing and amenities are at least frightening, if not discouraging, especially since national resources are extremely limited.

The fourth and final policy implication is the *long-term* versus the short-term view as to where a nation's resources shall be invested most beneficially. This does not apply particularly to the larger new countries but is applicable to the more numerous small new countries, and especially to those with only a primate city. Although the pressure to allocate resources to one existing urban area of most newly developing countries is almost irresistible, a question which continually lurks in the minds of many persons responsible for these decisions is whether it is preferable and possible to risk the short-term consequences of what would appear to be a better alternative in the long run, namely, the development of a *group* of cities rather than one or two. There would be difficulties in attempting to diversify the investments of time, money, energy, and staff in endeavoring to develop concurrently several urban centers rather than one or two. Nevertheless it is apparent that in large countries—although it is only slightly less true of smaller ones—there is a sound logic involved in the long-term consideration to attempt to develop more than one or a very small number of urban centers. If, as is assumed will be the case, the small, newly developing nation survives and prospers, it is extremely likely that it will require additional urban centers to service the growth of the new economy and to carry forward the programs of the new government. These additional centers are always more difficult to develop once heavy investments have been made in only one urban area.

Various cultural stresses and strains are associated with the development of urbanization in newly developing countries, an urbanization which more often than not is both discordant to the predominantly rural culture and atypical to the limited urban culture which exists before the formation of a new nation. Exceptions occur in those cases where some urbanization is developed under colonial auspices, or in the rare instances where urbanization, such as among the Yoruba, develops indigenously.

An observer ordinarily thinks of the impact of an urban area upon the countryside's rural and village customs. There is also an obverse to this relationship which should not be overlooked. If you reverse the situation, the transplantation of rural ways of life into the urban context—even if these ways of life survive for only a short time—may be considered to be functionally discordant to urbanism. The conflict of rural practice and custom with an established urban way of doing things may introduce complications that could well be avoided.

Insofar as the introduction of discordant elements in either direction—*i.e.*, from urban to rural or rural to urban—takes place, it is probable that what survives from the rural transplant of culture has suitability or functional value in the new context. In any case, it is not likely to impede the functioning of the society for a very long period. Changes will occur, but presumably those that will emerge are likely to have the highest functional value to the new urban culture.[4]

Comparative Analysis of Urbanization

Systematic comparison of urbanization would ideally rest on accurate and complete statistical data, not only for the growth and characteristics of cities, but also for the other critical features of developing countries. Though some of the data on cities have been presented in Chapter One, and materials on the correlates of urbanism may be available in the near future,[5] wide generalization is scarcely possible at this juncture. One alternative is the use of a typology, which follows a middle course between "universal" relations and the description of isolated cases.

TYPOLOGY OF URBAN AREAS

Despite the difficulties of scarce data, wide ranges in scales and types of urbanization, and significant differences in stages of national development, classification is essential.

Origins of Variations

Among the factors which must be taken into account in attempting to construct a typology of urbanization in newly developing countries is that of the auspices under which urbanization in a particular country begins, reaches its major period of growth, and continues at the present time. The type of city that results, for example, from a history of indigenous urbanization—as with the Yoruba in the case of Nigeria—as compared with urbanization stimulated under colonial auspices, is

[4] See Robert Redfield and Milton B. Singer, "The Cultural Role of Cities," *Economic Development and Cultural Change,* 3 (October 1954), 53–73.

[5] Kingsley Davis and Hilda Hertz, "Patterns of World Urbanization."

readily observable as evidenced in size of city, type of development, density of population, characteristics of housing and facilities, and so on. In most newly developing countries there is only a brief history of indigenous urbanization. Rather, most of the existing urbanization appears to have begun under colonial interests and sponsorship. There are exceptions to this generalization as, for example, in the case of Cairo and some of the larger urban agglomerations of Communist China.

There are even variations in the urbanization which took place under colonial auspices. As Kingsley Davis points out, the Spanish colonial policy of exploitation extended even to control over the kinds of trade which South American outposts could conduct with one another. Davis cites as an illustration the case of Buenos Aires, which was prohibited from such trade:

> Two hundred years after it was founded, Buenos Aires still only had 25,000 inhabitants, whereas New York City, the same length of time after its founding by the Dutch, had approximately 150,000. The speed with which Buenos Aires, once its shackles were removed, surpassed Lima also indicates the depressing effects of the early restrictions on the Argentine city.[6]

Similar preferential treatment in terms of contacts from time to time characterized the operation of the East Indies Company.

Some of the variations in the types of urban areas in newly developing countries also arose by virtue of special situations vis-à-vis trade routes by sea that placed certain cities, such as Hong Kong and Singapore, in particularly good locations for growth.

Another factor which affected the type of city which emerged was whether the development of nationhood followed colonial experience or indigenous development. In other words, it has made a very great difference, in terms of types of urbanization, as to whether development of a city has been established in a particular stage of the indigenous-colonial-nationhood sequence and context, since this would affect not only the physical pattern of the city but also the type of growth involved. Similarly, the importance of the resources of a country, in terms of their potential for exploitation or national development, inevitably has had an impact on the extent and character of urbanization. Illustrations include West Africa's smaller countries that have limited tributary areas on which they can depend for resources to supplement or otherwise affect their growth.

[6] Kingsley Davis, "Colonial Expansion and Urban Diffusion in the Americas," *International Journal of Comparative Sociology,* 1 (March 1960), 51.

The Primate City Case

One of the common classification categories for urbanization in newly developing countries has been that of the primate city.[7] A city is a primate city in a circumstance in which there is one surpassingly large city in a country as compared with all other urbanization. The existence of primate cities has not been limited to non-Western areas. Several examples of primate cities at different periods in the histories of the countries involved include Stockholm for Sweden, Oslo for Norway, Paris at one time for France, Brussels for Belgium, Venice and Rome at different periods in the history of Italy, and Athens for Greece.[8] Bert F. Hoselitz points out that most of the major functions for these countries became concentrated in these cities at a very early stage in their development. He notes that some of the claims that refer to the parasitic nature of these cities are: (1) that they swallow up investment, (2) absorb manpower, (3) dominate the cultural pattern, (4) have a deleterious effect on the development of other cities, and (5) tend to have a high consumption rate as compared with production rate. He examines all of these claims and observes, quite properly, that it may very well be that a country in an early stage of its development can only afford or support one great city. Hoselitz also indicates that it is very difficult to predict when, and under what circumstances, a primate city may decrease in importance in a particular country. It is apparent that the existence of a primate city case must vary with the size of a country. It would not be expected, for example, that a country as large as India would be characterized by the existence of a single primate city as are certain West African countries, although the classic case of Nigeria must not be overlooked because for a long period of time this country has included a number of cities of substantial size. Brian J. L. Berry indicates that primate cities are likely to be characteristic of (1) countries which until recent times were politically or economically dependent on other countries, (2) small countries which once had extensive areas, or (3) countries where the economies of scale are such as

[7] Mark Jefferson, "The Law of the Primate Cities," *Geographical Review,* **29** (April 1939), 226–32. Also, Rhoads Murphey, "New Capitols of Asia," *Economic Development and Cultural Change,* **5** (April 1957), 216–43, dealing particularly with Karachi, Delhi, Colombo, Rangoon, Bangkok, Kuala Lumpur, Singapore, Djakarta, and Manila; and Norton S. Ginsburg, "The Great City in Southeast Asia," *American Journal of Sociology,* **60** (March 1955), 455–62. See also Surinder K. Mehta, "Some Demographic and Economic Correlates of Primate Cities: A Case for Revaluation," *Demography,* **1,** No. 1 (1964), 136–47.

[8] Bert F. Hoselitz, "Urbanization and Economic Growth in Asia," mimeographed for Congress for Cultural Freedom Conference on Problems of Economic Growth, Tokyo (April 1–6, 1957), pp. 4ff.

not to require cities of intermediate sizes.[9] The implications of the existence of primate cities in newly developing countries have been explored elsewhere in this study; the extent of their existence is indicated in the data presented in Chapter One.

Selected Classical Typologies

There have been many other attempts to construct a classification or typology of urban areas in newly developing countries. Henri Pirenne divided cities into two major groups: (1) political-intellectual centers, such as Delhi, Quito, and Peiping and (2) economic centers such as Bombay, Guayaquil, and Shanghai.[10] This is a simple enough classification but is not usable for purposes of ordering the wide variety of urbanization in newly developing countries at the present time.

Hoselitz has attempted a broad classification in terms of "generative" and "parasitic" cities. He classifies a city as generative "if its impact on economic growth is favorable, *i.e.*, if its formation and continued existence and growth is one of the factors accountable for the economic development of the region or country in which it is located." He classifies a city as parasitic if "it exerts an opposite impact." [11] Hoselitz makes it clear that the periods during which cities are parasitic or generative may vary a great deal, and may shift from one type to another. He also notes that some cities may be generative in terms of their immediate environs but parasitic for the larger areas which they dominate. As in the case of Pirenne's simple classification, the generative-parasitic classification also has the limitation of not being detailed enough to handle all the variety of cities found in newly developing countries.

The Pirenne and Hoselitz classifications have been modified substantially by Robert Redfield and Milton Singer, who classify cities in terms of their cultural role as "orthogenetic" and "heterogenetic" as follows: orthogenetic—"carrying forward into systematic and reflective dimensions an old culture," as compared with heterogenetic—"creating of original modes of thought that might have authority beyond or in conflict with old cultures and civilizations." [12] Redfield and Singer refer to the former classification, cities of orthogenetic transformation, as being cities of a moral order, and the latter, cities of heterogenetic transformation, as

[9] Brian J. L. Berry, "City Size Distribution and Economic Development," *Economic Development and Cultural Change,* 9 (July 1961), 573–88.

[10] Henri Pirenne, *Belgian Democracy: Its Early History* (Manchester: Manchester University Press, 1915), esp. Chap. iii, pp. 55ff.

[11] B. F. Hoselitz, "Generative and Parasitic Cities," *Economic Development and Cultural Change,* 3 (April 1955), 279.

[12] Robert Redfield and Milton Singer, "The Cultural Role of Cities," *Economic Development and Cultural Change,* 3 (October 1954), esp. 56–57.

being cities of a technical order. As Redfield and Singer recognized, the same city may include both cultural roles. This, therefore, also becomes an interesting, but not entirely usable, classification because of its inability to differentiate among wide variations in urbanization.

Another classification of urbanization into "pre-industrial," "industrial," and "metropolitan" has been undertaken by Philip M. Hauser, who defines the categories as follows:

> The pre-industrial town is undoubtedly of great cultural significance. It is the seat of government, the country's religious center and the home of scientific and spiritual creative activity; but from the economic standpoint it is only very loosely connected with the territory that provides it with sustenance, and conducts an incipient interarea trade, without showing a clearly defined territorial division of labor.
>
> The industrial town, in contrast, is characterized by the existence of this territorial division of labor, organized around its manufacturing production. As has justly been observed, the technical basis of this organization is a socially centripetal force of steam-driven machinery and its transmission gear and belt system. The metropolitan city displays some of the same characteristics as the industrial town, in intensified form, but, on the other hand, it is based on a different technology. Steam-driven machinery is succeeded by the combustion engine and electricity, which figure in all their fields of application—production, communications and transport—as a socially centrifugal force which once again allows the population to spread out towards the countryside.[13]

Unfortunately this classification has some of the same limitations as the others to which reference has already been made.

It would be most helpful if it were possible to construct a fully usable typology of urbanization in newly developing countries. The task is a complex one, and although perhaps it is not hopeless, the results appear strained and inadequate. The variety of urbanization in newly developing countries appears to be such that various permutations and combinations of classification systems are necessary so that one may comprehend the complete range of phenomena. In this study no attempt has been made to explore, in an exhaustive fashion, all of the typologies or classification systems for urban areas. However, it is clear from those that have been examined that a really useful typology has yet to be devised. Rather, it would seem to be important to view urbanization in newly

[13] Philip M. Hauser, ed., *Urbanization in Latin America,* proceedings of a seminar sponsored jointly by the Bureau of Social Affairs of the United Nations, the Economic Commission for Latin America, and UNESCO (in cooperation with the International Labor Organization and the Organization of American States) on urbanization problems in Latin America, Santiago, Chile, July 6–18, 1959 (Paris: UNESCO, 1961), pp. 23–24 (hereafter referred to as UNESCO, *Latin America*).

developing countries from several *different* perspectives and to classify, where necessary for particular purposes, in terms of size of urban area, whether a country is a primate-city country by the extension of industrialization apparent in the urbanization, and by the other characteristics referred to at the beginning of this discussion. Though this conclusion may be considered a retreat from the problem, we are hopeful that there may be devised at some future date a comprehensive classification system that will incorporate the full range of urbanization in newly developing countries. Perhaps the attempt to construct a typology is a fruitless way of approaching the complexity of urbanization in these countries. Explicating analytical relations among the range of variables, as simply as possible, as complexly as necessary, may be the answer.[14]

INDUSTRIALIZATION AND URBANIZATION

The relationship between industrialization and urbanization in newly developing countries has been the subject of much research and extensive publication.[15]

Many different aspects of industrialization as related to urbanization in newly developing countries are discussed throughout this study. It is perhaps appropriate here to deal only, and briefly, with the broader general question of the relationship between industrialization and urbanization.

There has been much casual observation to the effect that there is a direct correlation between the development of urbanization and the development of industrialization, each being cited by different authors as being the "cause" of the other. Although there is often a coincidence of industrialization and urbanization, the causal relationships are not at

[14] The author is indebted to Wilbert E. Moore for this comment.

[15] A full bibliography of the most significant analyses of the relationship between industrialization and urbanization is too lengthy for inclusion here. Certain well-known publications related to this subject, however, are as follows: Bert F. Hoselitz and Wilbert E. Moore, eds., *Industrialization and Society* (Paris and the Hague: UNESCO and Mouton, 1963); Wilbert E. Moore and Arnold S. Feldman, eds., *Labor Commitment and Social Change in Developing Areas* (New York: Social Science Research Council, 1960); Wilbert E. Moore, *Industrialization and Labor: Social Aspects of Economic Development* (Ithaca and New York: Cornell University Press, 1951); Ralph Braibanti and Joseph J. Spengler, eds., *Tradition, Values and Socioeconomic Development* (Durham, N.C.: Duke University Press, 1961); R. B. Textor, P. N. Prabhu, A. F. A. Husain, and M. B. Deshmukh, *The Social Implications of Industrialization and Urbanization: Five Studies of Urban Populations of Recent Rural Origin in Cities of Southern Asia* (Calcutta: UNESCO Research Center on the Social Implications of Industrialization in Southern Asia, 1956); Richard L. Meier, *Science and Economic Development: New Patterns of Living* (New York: John Wiley & Sons, Inc., 1956).

all clear. The subject is somewhat confused by the fact that certain common features of industrialization—such as the extensive division of labor —are found in countries that are relatively unindustrialized. For example, it would be extremely difficult to find a more detailed, intensive, and comprehensive division of labor than is involved in the caste system which persisted over thousands of years in the absence of any significant degree of urbanization and industrialization.

In spite of the difficulty and lack of success in establishing close or causal relationships between industrialization and urbanization, it still is evident that there is a substantial impact of industrialization on many aspects of urbanization. Industrialization is likely to affect, in a very significant way, not only the rate of growth of particular urban areas but also the type of growth in urbanization, as well as the relative level of economic development involved in urbanization.

It is apparent that early stages of industrialization in newly developing countries may be characterized by focus on manufacturing of consumer goods, involving mostly light industrial operations. Later stages involving heavier industry are likely to be more directly related, locationwise, to the existence of raw materials and sources of power.[16] It is because of the locations at which these different levels of industrial development can take place efficiently, the ramifications of the appearance of industrialization, and the extent of the process, that planners for economic development in newly developing countries have a very high interest in the industrialization process itself. These planners customarily examine the course of industrialization in Western countries with great care, but it has never been clearly shown that it is possible to make reliable projections as to what will happen in a newly developing country on the basis of the experience of Western nations where industrialization began under quite different circumstances. The importance of industrialization to economic planning for a nation cannot be underrated, and officials responsible for such planning are very much aware of the influx of population into urban areas in proportions generally too great to be accommodated by the number of jobs available. The customary posture adopted under these circumstances is to seek as rapid industrialization as possible to provide employment.

There are clearly many difficulties involved in undertaking this development of industry. Among other things, industry depends partly—particularly when extensive and heavy—on a related "infrastructure," *i.e.*, supporting light industrial activities and specialized services. Although

[16] See discussion by Philip M. Hauser in UNESCO, *Asia and the Far East*, pp. 6ff.

the labor force in newly developing countries is readily amenable to training for industrial occupations, the process requires a considerable period of time and cannot proceed to sophisticated levels over a short period. In addition, there is a problem of training middle-range personnel to handle management and administrative aspects of industrial undertakings. But it is the infrastructure in particular which tends to substantially influence both the location of industry and the extent of industrialization in newly developing countries.

In general, only a small number of cities are able to undertake much industrialization in the early stages of economic development. These are likely to be the large cities where the probability is highest that several industries will be able to share the expensive overhead of power plants, water supply, sewage treatment plants and other utilities as well as the related skills and services which must be provided to supplement the industries themselves. It is apparent that these facilities, services, and equipment are not available in village environments. Industrialization undertaken in such decentralized locations inevitably is very expensive because of the necessity of underwriting both the cost of establishing the industry and providing the infrastructure. To this must be added the cost of getting finished goods to the consumers in the large urban areas which, in a newly developing country, are most likely to have the largest market for manufactured goods. The usual result is that a relatively small number of cities, or even one city in the case of primate city countries, dominates the early industrialization resources of a newly developing country.

The relationship between industrialization and urbanization is complicated by the fact that there is not necessarily a suitable, or most appropriate or optimum, timing in the rate of urbanization and the rate of industrialization, even assuming they proceed at equivalent levels. Contemporary urbanization almost invariably precedes industrialization except in obvious cases such as the establishment of "New Towns" for the erection of steel mills and similar installations. One of the major development questions in these countries is whether and when it may be possible for industrialization—in terms of producing jobs—to catch up with urbanization. The narrowing of this gap is one of the prime objectives of economic development planners, and has become so important that it is likely to dominate the allocation of resources in early stages of development.

The subject has many ramifications, too detailed to be examined here. The crucial importance of careful planning of industrialization for the future is suggested by Wilbert E. Moore who observes:

The correlation of industrialization and urbanization is not perfect in any event. Large cities have developed in many countries as "cultural" and government centers, as "overgrown villages" of agriculturists, as residences of absentee landlords, and as centers of trade. Much of the future economic growth will probably be centered in these urban areas, simply because they are there and provide both pools of labor and various public facilities. Continued urbanization, including the growth of new population centers, is to be expected.[17]

The ramifications of the relationship between industrialization and urbanization are obviously significant in the question of creating a typology or classification of urban areas.

MORPHOLOGY OF URBAN AREAS

Knowledge of the morphology of urban areas in newly developing countries facilitates the understanding of the general characteristics of cities and their implications for these countries. In Chapter Four considerable attention is devoted to the *development* of urban areas, various growth patterns, ecological processes at work, patterns of land use, values, and land ownership, as well as general questions related to supplying facilities and services. Our present purpose, however, is best served by an illustration of urbanization in a newly developing country, recognizing that there are considerable and significant variations involved elsewhere but assuming that this case suggests the ranges in the morphology of an urban area.

This study, accordingly, turns to a discussion of the morphology of the city of Delhi-New Delhi, India, as incorporating most of the features of urbanization in newly developing countries, particularly in large-scale cities and those that have been exposed both to indigenous and colonial growth influences, as well as subsequent growth during the period of national emergence. Among other things that will be observed in this case study is that, lacking a national tradition of urbanization, it was natural that Western forms and ways of doing things would be imitated. This practice was possibly influenced by participation of foreigners and the idea that Western urban forms would be relevant to the forthcoming urbanization in these countries. The question remains as to whether it is possible and satisfactory to "transplant" patterns from Western urbanization to these countries and have them satisfactorily meet different requirements.

[17] Wilbert E. Moore, "The Social Framework of Economic Development," in Braibanti and Spengler, eds., *Tradition, Values, and Socioeconomic Development* (Durham, N.C.: Duke University Press, 1961), p. 74.

The following case study presents a moment in time of a major urban area undergoing rapid change.[18]

A Case Study of Delhi-New Delhi, India

INTERNAL CONTRASTS IN INDIAN CITIES

Constructing generalizations for very large Indian urban areas is only slightly less difficult than doing the same thing for all Indian urbanization.[19] The range of phenomena sometimes seems to defy the effort. This

Table 8

Intra-urban Passenger Movement Classified by Mode of Conveyance, Delhi, 1957 *

Mode	Passenger trips handled	
	Number	Per cent
Bicycles	400,000	36.0
Delhi Transport Undertaking bus	240,000	21.0
Tongas (two-wheeled horsecarts)	136,000	12.6
Private cars	110,500	10.1
Taxis	60,000	4.4
Scooter rickshaws (motorized)	45,000	4.0
4-seater motor rickshaws	42,400	3.8
Cycle rickshaws	42,400	3.8
Private buses	15,000	1.3
Tramways	14,000	1.2
Motorcycles and scooters	12,500	1.0
Railways	6,000	0.4
Total	1,123,800	100.0

* *Source: Origin and Destination Survey of Traffic in Urban Delhi—1957,* and Delhi Transport Undertaking data for 1957; adapted with corrections from Delhi Development Authority, *Draft Master Plan for Delhi* (1960), Vol. I, p. 138, Table 19.

[18] Reproduced with minor changes and additions from the following: Gerald Breese, "Urban Development Problems in India," *Annals of the Association of American Geographers,* **53** (September 1963), esp. pp. 254–65.

[19] Space limitations suggest that the reader be referred to two published bibliographies: (1) Bert F. Hoselitz, "A Survey of the Literature on Urbanization in India," in Roy Turner, ed., *India's Urban Future* (Berkeley and Los Angeles: University of California Press, 1962), pp. 425–43, first published in *Annals of the Association of American Geographers,* **49** (June 1959), 223–31, and (2) John E. Brush, "The Morphology of Indian Cities," in Turner, ed., *India's Urban Future,* pp. 57–70, in which Brush independently arrived at observations similar to those reported below.

is an especially trying problem in the case of India's largest cities, since their sites, situations, and degrees of foreign influence vary widely. For example, the variations in site characteristics of Calcutta, Madras, Delhi, and Bombay raise doubts as to whether any comparisons are possible. It is surprising, however, to observe how many similarities in urban phenomena are derivable in spite of such diverse characteristics.

One of the most noticeable features of large Indian cities is their combination of very high population density in relatively small areas and relatively low population density over other large areas. This phenomenon is accentuated in the Delhi area by the presence of New Delhi, a special case that will be discussed later. In addition to the small area-high density, low density-large area contrast, these same large Indian urban areas are also marked by burgeoning areas of temporary settlement, usually either in or near the Old City, or at the periphery of the urban area. These are the "bustee" or "tin-town" agglomerations about which more will be said later.

Also part of the "general picture" of the large Indian urban area is the contrasting road and circulation pattern. Leaving details for discussion elsewhere, it is sufficient for the present to note the sharp contrast between the convoluted Old City matrix (Figure 7) and the combined gridiron-diagonal features of circulation channels in newer areas.

The railroad pattern is of some special interest. As in European cities, the railroads entered large urban areas at a relatively recent date. Consequently, they seldom penetrate the Old City area, but thrust inward as far as possible to establish stations, goods yards, etc., then loop around what was then the built-up area and have been subsequently enclosed by later growth.

The transportation "mix" in large Indian urban areas further complicates circulation (Table 8). Those who walk from place to place make the vast majority of trips and have a profound effect on the distribution of land use. For those who travel by other means and move goods from place to place otherwise than on their backs, the possible modes are many and varied, and change with time (Table 9). Animal and vehicular transportation ranges from the sluggish camel and donkey

---

This analysis is based largely on the writer's fifteen-month experience in 1957–1958 while coordinator of a Ford Foundation consulting team of seven persons assisting in the preparation of the Delhi (India) Regional Master Plan. See also Pradyumna Prasad Karan, "The Pattern of Indian Towns: A Study in Urban Morphology," *Journal of the American Institute of Planners,* 23 (1957), 70–75. Among others, R. L. Singh has written extensively on North Indian cities.

The best and most up-to-date discussion of urbanization in India is Roy Turner, ed., *India's Urban Future* (Berkeley and Los Angeles: University of California Press, 1962).

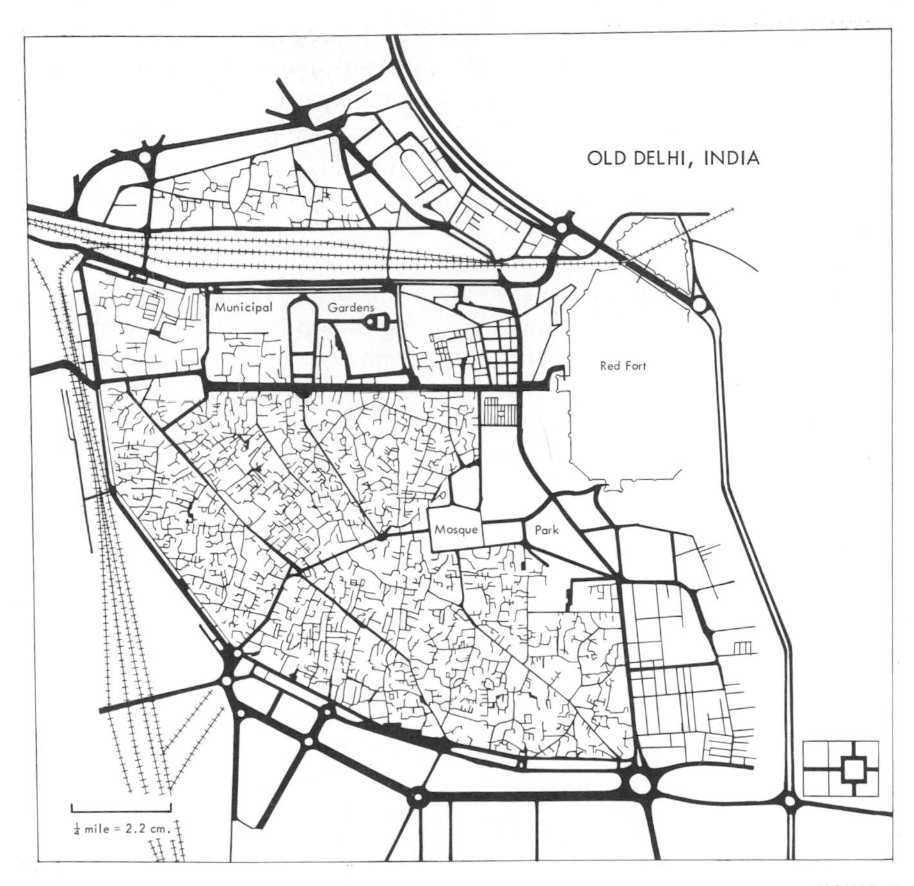

FIGURE 7

Old Delhi, India—Circulation

Source: Gerald Breese, "Urban Development Problems in India," Annals of the Association of American Geographers, **53** *(September 1963), 256.*

to the speeding truck and the rapid commuter train, as in Bombay. Between these are the tonga cart, pedicab, motorcycle rickshaw, bicycle, oxcart, taxi and private automobile, trucks of various kinds, handcart, bus and streetcar, to mention the chief modes of transportation. This melange of facilities, sharing the right-of-way in generally uncontrolled fashion, is both the product and the creator of the typically high mix of land uses in Indian urban areas, especially in the Old City sections.

The result of these combinations is a congested flow pattern producing apoplectic dismay among visiting foreign traffic experts. Yet the reasons for this mix of facilities are not hard to find. In the Old City context, where distances are not great and individual bulk movements are not large, there is in fact an undeniable kind of efficiency in cheap, slow-moving, low-cubage transport able to negotiate the convoluted street system. Longer distance and larger bulk movements are correspondingly forced onto the few major streets in the search for speed, generally a futile search since these streets are seldom effectively reserved for such traffic. In newer areas, where street patterns and design more nearly approximate those in European countries, there is a corresponding increase in speed of movement, modified however, by the necessity of joint use by vehicles moving at vastly different rates of speed.

For the urban planner these circumstances raise a variety of questions: how to segregate traffic, whether it is possible—or desirable—to recommend a union bus terminal, to what extent it is practicable to anticipate a rational pattern of differentiated land uses and functional areas, and so on.

Such questions automatically raise the subject of land use. There are two approaches possible here: (1) to study the various categories of land use as distributed throughout the entire area; (2) to analyze the different parts or components of the urban area (Old City, Cantonment, etc.). Both approaches are necessary; ideally, of course, they should be covered concurrently.

LAND USE

The highly mixed land use in Indian urban areas differs markedly from the usual segregation of land uses in Anglo-American cities. This appears to be the result of a long history of compact development and the continuing necessity of walking between places of residence and places of work or enjoyment.

Commercial

Commercial land use in Indian urban areas bears little resemblance to that of Anglo-American cities. The Anglo-American central business district, with its highly peaked and use-intensive development at a focal point, has as its Indian Old City counterpart a concentration of commercial uses in a more diffuse focal area. There is relatively little indication of "100 per cent location" identification. In some cases this is partly a result of there being no one small area into which all access roads and public transport lead and thus no push toward site-piling. Generally speaking, individual business sites are small, many shops being only a few feet wide. The small size of units permits lower-cost sharing of site

Table 9

Number of Registered Auto, Human Traction, and Animal-drawn Vehicles in Urban Delhi, 1947 and 1957–1958 *

Type of vehicle	1947	1957
Motorcars	6,414	10,281
Motorcycles and scooters	1,842	5,715
Stage carriers (buses)	330	1,023
Scooter rickshaws	No data	1,005
Taxicabs and tourist cars	262	1,391
Trucks		
Public carriers	No data	No data
Private carriers	671	2,191
School buses and government vehicles	284	543
Total	9,803	22,149
	1947–1948	**1957–1958**
Tongas (two-wheeled horsecarts)	3,311	3,034
Rehras (two-wheeled horsecarts for goods)	1,109	1,075
Bullock carts	3,526	3,491
Handcarts	663	2,856
Cycle rickshaws	250	700
Cycles	No data	146,966
Total	8,859	158,122

* *Sources:* Auto vehicles–State Motor Transport Controller's Office, Delhi; Human and animal–Municipal Corporation Officials. Data selected, and totals corrected, from Delhi Development Authority, *Draft Master Plan for Delhi* (1960), Vol. I, p. 125, Tables 4, 5.

and shop rentals, so that what otherwise might be impractically small scales of operation and volumes of business can survive. It is not uncommon to find manufacturing and sale of the same article combined in one establishment.

Generally, in larger cities, various types of goods and services are likely to be sorted out into specialized areas that together form the *chauk.* Many such specialized parts of the chauk area are quite small, but others may develop into substantial subcenters, such as grain exchanges or cloth markets. Interrelated shops and services tend to gravitate to one another's vicinity. The shopping process becomes a matter of numerous stops since each dealer usually handles a very limited line of goods.

Inventories tend to be low, but where the character of goods requires it, the inventory is stored in nearby *godowns* (warehouses). The scale of operations and the limited capital involved require frequent small-lot deliveries from godowns to wholesalers. This practice, combined with the diffuse nature of the chauk, creates certain planning difficulties as, for example, in centralizing truck terminals for pickup and delivery.

In the large cities, the old chauk is supplemented—and often overshadowed—by the younger Anglo-American style "central" business district. Sometimes this adjoins the Old City center, as in Bombay; in other cases, as in Delhi, some distance separates the two "centers." The new centers aim to be reasonable facsimiles of their foreign models but are on a smaller scale, and tend to be less compact and mixed with other kinds of land use. Often, but not invariably, there is a close relationship between these central business areas and the railway station and Anglo-American style residential area.

One other central shopping facility requires incidental notice—the large *covered* shopping complex consisting of dozens of small shops under one roof, and more or less organized into specialty areas by type of merchandise. The Sir Stuart Hogg Market in Calcutta is an example. These are somewhat reminiscent of the Middle Eastern *souk,* but the shops are bunched rather than strung out in a line.

Wholesaling of foods is generally located well outside the main chauk, though the location has to be fairly easily accessible to all major routes from the countryside, since most of the produce is grown in areas directly tributary to the urban area and is brought in fresh. The produce market is often found in conjunction with railway sidings. Where cities have outgrown the capacity of the Old City produce center, or have extended their built-up limits over considerable distances, authorized or, more often, unauthorized outlying produce markets tend to be set up at less frequent but regular intervals. For most families, lack of refrigeration facilities and limited income necessitate daily shopping, thus placing a premium on markets located within walking distance of homes.

Throughout the Old City, and in more localized spots in newer areas, there are some minor subcenters and independent retail units having very restricted service areas. These facilities are supplemented by countless hawkers and sidewalk merchants with no site overhead costs. With the single exception of residence, commercial uses are the most ubiquitous. Only in British-built urban areas is there anything approaching the degree of separation of commercial and residential land use which has become almost a fetish in American cities.

Industrial

Industrial activity may—and does—appear almost anywhere in an Indian urban area, there being little tradition of effective enforcement of control over its location. As much of small-scale handcrafting has gradually changed into industrial production, and as the demand has grown for goods that are most efficiently produced in large-scale operations, industry has taken root in diverse parts of Indian urban areas.

It is true that there are some planned industrial estates in India, and that there are some cases where large industrial units, in particular, have been located rationally from every point of view. In the very large city—our primary interest here—this is the exception, rather than the rule, though the policy for the future envisions gradual improvement in this direction.

The great bulk of industry in Indian urban areas is in the Old City area and its dense appendages or overflow areas just outside. Most of it is small scale, in terms of both labor force and capital. More often than not, operations are carried on in converted structures or others somewhat unsuited to such use. In either case, they tend not to provide for expansion; frequently even the existing scale of operations forces encroachment on adjoining streets and into nearby buildings. In cases where an industry had a small beginning, but grew very rapidly, its expansion into contiguous areas has often resulted in general disregard for the invaded areas, creating both unattractive environs and inefficient factory layout. The one big advantage to randomly distributed manufacturing is that, in theory at least, it should reduce the time and cost of the journey to work, an important factor for low-income labor working long hours. Whether, in fact, workers actually are drawn from the nearby area is still uncertain, there having been virtually no research on the subject.

Many inefficiencies follow from the limited equipment available, the more or less haphazard distribution of industry, and its generally small scale. For example, it appears that many of the Anglo-American patterns of linkage among various industries must be effected in Indian urban areas with additional expense and inefficiency, because the various phases of production are conducted at separate points, or because of dependence on a small number of marginal firms for ancillary services, the failure of any one to do its job having repercussions all along the line. This is not to imply that *all* Indian industry is plagued with these difficulties—for some of it is highly efficient.

The task of the urban planner is to propose practicable and gradual steps—for change will of necessity be very slow—in the direction of more efficient location of industrial land use consistent with other urban functions. Before this is possible, much more research is required to understand existing and potential industrial land-use patterns.

Residential

Variations of residential patterns will be discussed in more detail below in connection with specific parts of the urban area. Here only a few background observations will be suggested.

Perhaps the most important feature of residential development is the great range in population density. *Gross* densities in Delhi, for example, range from an average of 13.16 persons per acre in New Delhi to an average of 213.34 persons per acre in Old Delhi, figures which are somewhat misleading as to *net* density living conditions. Since gross densities include acreage devoted to railway yards, street areas, etc., the net densities are frequently much higher. In the case of Delhi, for example, Bopegomage [20] points out that in Kashmeregate Constituency the gross density is 74 persons per acre (ppa), while the net density is 299 ppa; in Jama-Masjid Constituency the gross density of 394 ppa becomes a net density of 1,128 ppa; in Roshanara-Extension Constituency the gross density of 85 ppa becomes a net density of 358 ppa; and in Ramnagar Constituency the gross density of 221 ppa becomes a net density of 420 ppa, etc. The significant factor, of course, is that these great variations in density occur in areas of mainly one- and two-story buildings. Where structures are higher, as in the case of Bombay's *chawls*,[21] densities soar even higher.

Recent calculations by R. Ellefsen,[22] of the University of California's International Urban Research organization, call attention to striking contrasts between densities of inner and peripheral wards in 13 large cities. In what he refers to as "British Period Developed Cities" (Bangalore, Bombay, Calcutta, and Madras) the differences in persons per inner and peripheral square mile range from 3:1 to 5:1; in "Pre-British Period Developed Cities" the ratios of inner to peripheral densities are approximately Ahmedabad 8:1, Allahabad 6:1, Banaras 8:1, Baroda 9:1, Delhi 13:1, Hyderabad 4:1, Kolhapur 5:1, Lucknow 4:1, and Poona 8:1.

From the urban planner's point of view, these variations in density represent such vast differences in amenity that every conceivable effort must be made to introduce adjustments. One of the possibilities under

[20] A. Bopegomage, *Delhi: A Study in Urban Sociology* (Bombay: University of Bombay, 1957), Table 6, p. 38. Table 14 on p. 69 provides data on number of houses, number of houses per acre, and number of persons per 100 houses, all data being for 1951.

[21] *Chawls* are three- to four-story structures, generally arranged so that each floor has two opposite rows of one-room apartments on either side of a central hall. Conversion or joint occupancy to accommodate more than one family is common.

[22] In a table distributed and discussed at the 1960 Seminar on Urbanization in India at Berkeley.

consideration for reducing inner ward densities is increasing the density of such very low density areas as New Delhi and Civil Lines. In New Delhi, for example, the lot sizes and the patterns of land occupancy are such as to permit relatively easy increases of density up to 75–90 persons per acre and still maintain a surprisingly high level of amenities. Such a procedure may be necessary to alleviate overcrowding and pressure on obsolescent structures, since the Anglo-American device of redevelopment is impracticable in the face of a necessity to preserve every barely habitable structure for the housing of the ever-increasing population, even without reducing the existing housing deficit.

Large Indian urban areas have never quite recovered from the influx of population incidental to Partition, later accentuated by the continuing flood of in-migrants from rural areas. As will be noted below, large numbers of these refugees and newcomers have been squatting on open land they do not own, or living in structures the owners are willing to overload with people, further increasing the density of the Old City and close-in areas that have the benefits of accessibility to whatever employment there may be. From the refugee's and newcomer's point of view, here is at least a place, however bad, to try for a new foothold. Their job-hunting success varies from Delhi to Calcutta.

These observations about land uses in Indian urban areas must be understood as representing the *general* case. In specific cities, it is necessary to point out the modifying influence of variations in topography (site), location with reference to other cities and the country (situation), historical period during which major city growth took place, and similar conditioning factors. No effort has been made here to detail all such variations, even among the large cities with which we are primarily concerned.

THE COMPONENTS OF LARGE INDIAN URBAN AREAS

A second illuminating approach to Indian urban areas is through analysis of the various parts of the urban complex: the Old (*i.e.*, indigenous) City, Civil Lines, government housing areas and cantonments, bastis and village enclaves, so-called "Western additions," and recent growth areas.

The Indigenous City

The fact that several of the very large Indian urban areas grew extensively under foreign influence somewhat complicates the consideration of their Old City component. However, the Indian urban areas under substantial British influence either had core Old Cities or subsequently developed areas with similar characteristics. Where the Old City served as the core of urban development, as in Delhi, that area may be considered as the real center of development, though subsequent events may have left it in a somewhat off-center position or have dwarfed it in importance, as in Bombay.

The characteristic features of Old Cities in our sample of large urban areas vary somewhat. Generally, the Old City is a mile or less in diameter, though it may, as in Delhi, house a great majority of the population. Originally—and sometimes to the present, as in the case of Delhi—the Old City was surrounded by walls pierced by a few gates. Heavily residential in character, the Old City nevertheless shares its limited space with other uses. The house tax assessment registers of Delhi, for example, reveal that in Delhi's walled city 42 per cent of its houses are put to nonresidential use, with 35 per cent having shops and 6 per cent industry godowns.[23]

Its street pattern reflects some of the original defense considerations, with a few transverse streets from one major gate to another. Occasionally a through street from a subsidiary gate leads to the main axes. The remainder of the Old City streets tend to be quite irregular in direction, length, width, and suitability for more than foot and animal traffic. A melange of convoluted streets, cul-de-sacs, alleys, and byways gives access to residences and commercial uses and much small industry encroaching or seeming to encroach on the public right-of-way.

Gates or doorways open to private residences and courtyards, or to *katras*.[24] The density of residence and the mixture of land uses is high, made more tolerable, perhaps, by the fact that residents may achieve some privacy from facing on internal courtyards, and not on the street. There is a considerable amount of segregation—some voluntary, some not—into small areal groupings, or into *mohallas* by caste, language group, geographical origin, religion (*e.g.*, Moslems in the vicinity of major mosques), and income group. Except for mosque areas and temple yards, there is virtually no public open space; indeed, even the streets are inadequate for the traffic and life they carry. Here, for the bulk of the population, is the core of the city. The foreigner, in an unfamiliar universe, finds it both hard to find his way, and hard to understand.

The walled Old City precincts have not been adequate to contain the population they have attracted, so adjoining areas have taken the

[23] Delhi [India] Development Authority, via Town Planning Organization, *Draft Master Plan for Delhi* (1960), Vol. I, text and drawings, p. 119.

[24] A *katra* is usually a group of single-room tenements facing on a courtyard or other enclosure that has access to the street by only one opening or gate.

surplus. Generally outside the wall there is some improvement of street patterns, but the interstices develop at densities rivaling those of the Old City on the other side of the wall.[25] Any attempts that might have been made to control land use have collapsed under mounting population pressure. Thus, dwelling units are frequently converted into shops and small factories; others are converted by subdivision to house more people. As might be expected, these Old City appendages have begun outside gates, but subsequently have taken over the Old City periphery in its entirety. They are extended farthest along major access roads, which seem invariably to become congested by commercial and other enterprises that illegally encroach on the right-of-way. This overflow area tends to remain the same in character as it moves outward to the end of walking distance from the central area. Quite commonly these areas are woefully short of adequate shopping facilities, sources of employment, open space, and even water and sewage facilities. Farther, or beyond some natural or man-made barrier, are found the more open and more affluent settlements to be described below.

Civil Lines

In sharp contrast to the Old City and its appendages, Civil Lines present an aspect of relative openness, green, order, and quiet. With relics of foreign government administration and the homes of the administrators formerly located here, Civil Lines seem sharply out of character with the Old Cities to which they were attached.

The Civil Lines street pattern, lot arrangement, and separation of land uses are formal and spacious importations. The rare tree in the Old City is mocked by the carefully tended—and irrigated, if necessary—greenery here. Even where parts of the Lines areas have fallen into neglect the impression is one of a more comfortable and inviting environment. At least that is the impression from the street side. Ancillary servant compounds may be no better than elsewhere.

Service facilities for the Lines often included an Indian market to

[25] Qadam Sharif in Delhi is typical of spillover areas that already require redevelopment: "The road and street system is confusing and inefficient. None of the major roads . . . [is] able to cope with the flow of traffic they attract. . . . Qadam Sharif measures 180 acres and is inhabited by 53,000 persons. The gross and net densities per acre are 294 and 558 persons respectively. . . . Roughly three fourths of the structures are in poor condition and excepting the recently built houses in Arya Nagar and Ram Nagar, all others are in dilapidated condition. Basic civic amenities are grossly inadequate. There are no private [water] taps for 67.1 per cent of the households, no latrines for 60.5 per cent and no electricity connections for 73.2 per cent. Public taps and latrines are few, and people use open spaces for defecation purposes." (Delhi Development Authority, *Draft Master Plan for Delhi,* Vol. II, appendices and drawings, p. 122.)

supply foodstuffs as a convenience to residents. If not in permanent quarters, such markets are temporarily set up in clearings.

The fate of Civil Lines areas since 1947 has varied. Some have been well preserved and remain attractive; more often the cost of upkeep and the pressures for accommodating a larger population have combined to induce decay. In other cases, parts of old Civil Lines areas have been adapted for nonresidential activities—Police Lines, hospitals, etc. From the planner's viewpoint, the Civil Lines, which are frequently close to the Old City, represent opportunities for increasing density to absorb the overcrowded Old City without compromising desirable amenities. It is not known just what portions of Civil Lines have been removed from public ownership, but insofar as they are still within government control, such development at higher densities could be expedited.

Cantonments

The Cantonments, or military reservations, are without doubt the single most voracious land eaters in Indian urban areas. Their thousands of acres are mostly held vacant for maneuvers, emergency camps, and similar military uses, in which the permanent cadre and troops are allotted an area for residential purposes. The layout of this portion is generally quite formalized and geometric, with a small market area serving as the center around which residential areas are assigned, the desirability of site being proportional to rank. The entire complex tends to be developed as a self-contained unit with outside contact mostly unnecessary.

The location and shape of the Cantonments may have profound effects on urban growth patterns. Where they are longitudinal to main travel arteries to the central city, they may not substantially alter growth direction but merely withhold land from urban expansion. Where they lie athwart expansion, they may either deflect or halt it. Insofar as the Cantonments lie relatively close in, and are in logical directions for urban growth, their disposition by conversion into other uses—more urban in character—is a matter of major interest to planners.

Special Areas

Other special areas, primarily for housing, commonly found in or near Indian urban areas include Railway Lines, Police Lines, and government housing complexes of various sorts, their names indicating the special occupation groups for which they are provided. Railway Lines are generally strung out along rights-of-way to provide special—often subsidized

—facilities for railway employees. In some cases they not only are unintegrated with surrounding development but also seriously lack necessary community services and facilities. Obvious related problems of interest to social scientists are the implications of communities "segregated" by occupations.

Similar questions arise in connection with government housing. The expansion of housing activity in the private sector has been extremely limited in Indian urban areas, purportedly because of the small percentage of the population able to participate in such a market. Responsibility for coping with the mounting housing deficit has thus largely depended on government and its bureaucracy. Accordingly there have been critical delays in the ponderous response to needs, compromise on standards (to stretch out the effect of available rupees), and not unexpected bureaucratic approaches to planning and allocation of units built. With reference to the last item, the prevailing tendency seems to have been to build for, and allocate to, government employees by branch of the government, type of job, rank, and income—a segregation procedure that raises some basic questions vis-à-vis a socialistic society, mobility potential, etc. In fact, the address of a government employee in government housing is an index to his status and income range.

In addition, government housing is frequently located some distance from place of work, or geographically isolated on sites for which there is no competition. Such housing is seldom, if ever, provided with adequate and well-designed shopping and market facilities (though plans often call for them), or with community centers. Servant quarters are either omitted entirely or patently inadequate. Attempts to integrate government housing into nearby areas are futile or entirely lacking.

Bustees

The prime evidence of massive housing deficits in urban India is the *bustee* (*busti*).[26] These *kachcha* (as distinct from *pukka*) or makeshift structures seem to appear overnight to become the abode of countless hundreds of thousands of squatters. They are found at the perimeters

[26] *Bustees* are small, temporary, and usually flimsy houses or huts built unauthorized on public or private lands by squatters. If they are made of castoff or poor materials they are *kachcha* construction and lack all amenities, often even windows. *Pukka* construction, *i.e.*, soundly built of good materials, is rare. Sanitary facilities are generally primitive, if they exist at all, and access to a safe water supply is difficult or nonexistent. Bustees are sometimes called *jhuggies* or *ahata* (as in Cawnpore).

In Delhi in 1959 there were reported to be 85 clusters of bustees of from 10 to 6,000 households; about one eighth, or 200,000 of the total population, were living in them. (Source: Delhi Development Authority, *Draft Master Plan for Delhi,* Vol. I, p. 115.)

of built-up urban areas, especially along major access routes; they spring up close to construction projects, and in cleared or undeveloped areas throughout the city; they occupy abandoned quarries and public parks, railway plazas, etc.; they pockmark residential areas ranging from slums to fine villa developments. They may be found in two's and three's, or in clusters of thousands. Most commonly one-room size, they produce very high densities in areas totally lacking in amenities. They are inhabited almost entirely by newcomers. Municipal officials make futile sorties aimed at their elimination and control, only to see their phoenix-like reappearance, and the survival of drumhead governing arrangements. Because of the housing shortage, they are ineradicable and continue to impede all efforts toward rational development.

Village Enclaves

The larger and more rapidly growing the urban area, the more likely it is to advance upon nearby villages, and either to embrace or obliterate them. If growth enfolds these villages, they may survive as enclaves until long after urban expansion has extended beyond them. In fact, it often proves excessively difficult to remove village enclaves, since they offer low-cost housing, become converted to marketplaces for the surrounding urban population, and provide a haven for furniture makers and other service operations. Stripped of their fields for agriculture, the village residents are forced to move elsewhere or attempt to enter the day- or servant-labor forces. Characteristically lacking in urban facilities such as public water supply, sewage, etc., the villages sometimes constitute a threat to the health of the city. From the circulation point of view, their irregular channels become congested with traffic and seldom join well with the superimposed street system of surrounding urban extensions. Muburakpur Kotla in Delhi might be taken as an example of these enclaves, albeit of somewhat higher grade than many others.

Other enclaves dot the urban landscape. "Fort" areas, relics of defense activities in bygone times, have generally managed to survive, though some have been used as quarries for ready-cut building blocks. They are located most often in the most congested quarters of the Old City, and if farsighted officials have successfully resisted pressures to fill them with municipal buildings, constitute what often is the only open space available. Religious precincts—temples, shrine areas, and mosque grounds—sometimes are large enough to constitute enclaves, islands of differentiation in the amorphous sea of surrounding congestion. For the urban planner, these enclaves offer hope as core centers for building community life.

"Suburban" Growth

As indicated above, private housing is only a small portion of Indian urban housing. It is almost exclusively concerned with high-income segments of the population. Even here custom building prevails, generally involving only a few housing units at a time. Nevertheless, together these activities are gradually producing peripheral imitations of foreign suburban-development patterns: spacious layout, single-family, two-story-plus structures, and larger street areas on modified gridiron-circulation systems. The population density is characteristically low, in spite of the common practice of adapting construction for temporary occupancy by an additional, renting family—a device to help defray the generally high costs of construction—with the hope that later rent will be discontinued and the owner can be the sole occupant. Servant quarters are often substandard, perhaps reflecting the anticipated decline of such staffing in the face of alternative work opportunities expected to accompany increasing industrialization.

Unfortunately there appears to be little system in the siting, planning, and development of these outlying areas. More often than not they are unbalanced communities with little or no provision for shopping and service facilities; surprisingly they often lie well beyond the service areas of water and sewage systems that they wishfully expected to be extended; they are commonly unprotected by zoning or other controls. Obviously they constitute development problems for the planner.

GROWTH AND PATTERN

Two general categories of observation require attention before we conclude the discussion. The first involves the difference between "indigenous" and "imported" patterns of development. The latter bear the stamp of Anglo-American concepts of street pattern, segregation of functional areas, and similar features of urban development familiar to Occidental inhabitants. Calcutta, Bombay, and Madras, for example, exhibit this legacy except at their very old cores. Where foreign influence has not been so great or so early as to shape the city, the more common indigenous pattern reflecting uncontrolled growth prevails, with mixed land use and smaller but more numerous foci of activity.

One other feature must be kept in mind in trying to understand growth *stages*. The rate of growth that has recently characterized Indian urbanization has offered very little opportunity, if indeed the opportunity has been taken into account at all, to regulate the expansion with reference to an overall plan.

In the course of this recent and rapid growth, Indian urban areas often bypass certain of the growth stages that were characteristic of developing Anglo-American urban areas. For example, the shift in predominant forms of transportation in Indian urban areas may be directly from animal and foot transportation to automobile, bus, and truck—without the intervening stages of local mass transportation by rail.

Another example of skipping stages in urban development characteristic of Anglo-American urban areas is in connection with forms of power available. Generally, when an urban area in a rapidly developing country begins to expand rapidly and to industrialize, it does so with the aid of electrical power. Because electrical power is relatively easy to distribute, its use has a quite different effect on distribution of industrial facilities and population from that of water power and site-generated steam power in the case of European and American cities. The latter forms of power can be characterized partly as concentrative in effect, particularly since at the time they were first employed there was no effective mass transportation to permit the dispersion of both industrial facilities and population.

Finally, it must be noted that the largest urban areas exhibit some of the "conurbation" features familiar in European-American experience. Greater Calcutta, for example, is an elongated conurbation along the Hooghly River. Bombay shows every indication of becoming, in a few decades, the center of a development that will curl around Bombay Harbor and north along the coast. Whether, and how often, similar conurbations develop will depend on factors not fully calculable, such as, for example, industrial location policies adopted by the planning commission of the government of India. If, for example, future national governmental policy should result in the directing of new industrial development to places outside the very large urban centers, this would obviously slow down the growth of Bombay, Calcutta, Madras, and Delhi. If, however, the experience of other countries is to be repeated in India, then the momentum already apparent in these cities will carry them to still greater size.

CONCLUSION

The primary purpose of this discussion has been to examine the form and structure of Indian urban areas insofar as they affect comprehensive planning for urban development. First, the internal contrasts in Indian cities have been explored. Second, and of major importance, the various categories of land use and the most significant components of typical large Indian urban areas have been studied to determine their origin, characteristics, and function as factors to be taken into account in comprehensive urban planning. Internal and external forces, practices, and policies affecting planning have been identified. In short, the crucial "givens" and "potentials" in large Indian cities have been put into the urban-*planning* context.

The secondary purpose, to examine the suitability of using the Delhi urban area for the preparation of a comprehensive master plan as a prototype for other Indian urbanization, has been approached somewhat incidentally. It is appropriate now to summarize the evidence on this point.

Two questions are involved: whether the Delhi area is typical of very large Indian urban areas, and whether it is representative of Indian urbanization in general. The latter may be more readily answered than the former. Although it has not been possible to present the facts here, from what is known [27] about other and smaller cities than Delhi, Calcutta, Bombay, and Madras, it must be recognized that smaller cities represent significant differences in kind and degree of urbanization from that of Delhi. To cite just one factor contributing to the differences: the larger cities such as Delhi, Calcutta, Bombay, and Madras have been subjected to much more foreign influence and settlement than have most other Indian cities. The result of this differential in influence, among other factors, is that the use of Delhi as a case for prototype planning for most Indian cities involves serious limitations. Nevertheless, there is rather great potential for transferability of research techniques and planning procedures among Delhi and other Indian cities.

The question of whether Delhi is more nearly suitable for use in prototype-comprehensive planning for India's very large cities is illuminated by considering its representativeness in view of similarities and dissimilarities among such cities. These very large urban areas—Delhi, Calcutta, Bombay, Madras—are different in the following respects: (1) their sites are vastly different, thus introducing some noncomparable planning problems; furthermore, the situation of Delhi is clearly not the same as the others; (2) in terms of areal components, Delhi is atypical partly because of the very large New Delhi area; (3) Delhi, more than the others, has dual central business districts of more nearly equal importance than in the case of the other cities; (4) the survival of the wall encirclement of Old Delhi serves as an atypical barrier not common to the other cities; (5) at present, at any rate, Delhi has more government housing than do the others; (6) the attitude toward industrialization is not the same in Delhi as elsewhere, and the prominence

[27] See fn. 19, pp. 55–56.

of government employment is different; and (7) Delhi does not have the same crucial problem of refugee settlement as Calcutta. On the other hand, Delhi and the other very large cities are quite comparable in terms of: (1) very rapid growth; (2) high mixture of land uses in older areas; (3) wide ranges in density of population; (4) large housing and amenity deficits; (5) except for heavy rail commuting in Bombay, many similarities in transportation and communication problems; (6) historically, heavy foreign influences on form and structure; (7) multiplicity of governing units in metropolitan area; and (8) uniformly low levels of public participation in the planning process. It is important to indicate that, although it has been impossible to introduce the detailed evidence here, all generalizations for Delhi have been checked against the main features of Bombay, Calcutta, and Madras and found to hold. Such checking, together with the judgment that the similarities among these very large cities are more significant for planning than the dissimilarities, suggest that, for the very large urban areas of India, Delhi is as nearly representative of all as any of the others. Any one, however, would inevitably be imperfect for this purpose.

This case study has the merit of being a detailed picture of a rapidly developing urban area in India. It has the limitation, however, of being a description of a somewhat different urbanization area from elsewhere in newly developing countries. Nevertheless, the major characteristics of the different portions, types, and kinds of urbanization may be considered roughly typical, although the nomenclature will vary and the proportions of urban areas devoted to each kind of use will be modified from country to country.

With such a typical case in mind we now turn our attention to the kinds of people who inhabit such areas and, subsequently, to the kinds of changes which have taken place and are expected to take place.

CHAPTER THREE

The Inhabitants

Familiarity with Western urbanization is grossly inadequate preparation for comprehending the full gamut of urban society in newly developing countries. This is particularly true for the characteristics of inhabitants of cities in such countries. Even casual observation shows, for example, that the similarities between Western urbanization and urbanization in these countries are minute. There appear to be vast disproportions in numbers and great gulfs in characteristics between the recent migrants coming into, and those persons with longer histories of living in, rapidly growing cities in terms of status and income levels, as well as cultural origins. Some migrants come from the "bush" and a much smaller number have such diverse backgrounds as a foreign education.

Perhaps a glimpse at the kinds of people found walking the streets and in the homes of urban areas in newly developing countries might be helpful. Picture the children, many of them bone-thin, shoeless, ragged, and unwashed, sometimes even unwanted, and often given the responsibility of overseeing younger siblings while their father and mother are desperately striving to make their way in the new urban society. These children may be highly conforming; on the other hand, thrown into a society which is unreal to them and with which they have had little experience, they often develop a kind of amoral stance, fearless except of the police, and highly unresponsive to their parents who are not only from another generation but also nonurban in experience as compared with their children.

Or take a look at the single young people who predominate among migrants to the urban area. They lack ties with the local society. They are likely to show a pallor from too little sleep, under too poor conditions, after too hard work at too low pay. They walk the streets silently, doing anything to escape the cramped quarters they must face as lodgers in other people's modest living areas. They range in experience from the naive, wondering new arrivals to those with a pseudo-sophisticated air of "old timers" who arrived a few months earlier. They have reached the urban area from countless points of origin after having paid their pittance of tribute for a bone-shaking ride on a produce truck. We see them endlessly walking, walking, walking, or squatting in a corner nibbling on their sparse portions of daily fare. They scramble on and off the ubiquitous "mammy wagons" of West Africa or doze in fretful sleep on a bullock cart returning from the urban market.

The women? Some toil up and down construction scaffolds, endless human chains of concrete carriers, with babies slung on their backs or deposited in a quiet corner with others of their kind. Or perhaps they are carrying lunches to their menfolk or collecting bundles of sticks for the fire or baskets of animal droppings to be dried for fuel. Most remarkably they are notable for their graceful posture under their heavy head burdens. In Egypt the women are dressed in black, in India in colorful saris; in West Africa they appear in blazing patterns of unpredictable color combinations. The few aged, on the contrary, are sitting stupefied in the sun, their mouths dripping betel juice through toothless smiles or snatches of conversation. They are rejects, often even in authority that has been stripped from them by urban ways; their sagging flesh and hollow eyes give clues not only to their present physical condition but also to the erosion of morale induced by their urban status.

If the migrants have arrived in a family group, the rural survival patterns appear quite unmistakably. For example, the wife walks the proper few steps behind her husband with a child clutching her skirts while another's head nods in sleep while being carried; they are going who knows where?

Have you seen their faces before? Have you not seen their faces everywhere in the cities of all newly developing countries?

WHO ARE THE INHABITANTS?

The current surge to the cities seems to be an urbanization quite different from the old-style urbanization, particularly with reference to the kinds of inhabitants. For example, the contemporary stream flows with enormously larger numbers of people; it involves migrants coming in with new types of relationships, not just as servants, as might have been the case in earlier days, but as potential factory workers, not just for an interim time, but to stay. Formerly these people were more directly under the control of Europeans who populated the larger centers; now this is much less often the case. They are the *nouveaux urbains* of the native population.

Migrant and Resident

And who are these migrants? What, in fact, is a migrant? When does a visitor to a great city become a resident there? When does a migrant become an urbanite? These are questions that have been explored in considerable detail by J. Clyde Mitchell.[1] Does a migrant or visitor to the city become an urbanite on the first day he arrives? Or if, having accumulated a small block of funds, he leaves after a short stay in the city, never to return, was he ever an urbanite? Or does he become an urbanite only when his children are born in the city and remain there? Is it only in the second generation that a person's family becomes urbanized? Who is an *inhabitant* of the city; when can this status be said to exist?

In some of the earlier stages of growth of urban areas in newly developing countries these were much more puzzling questions than at present, for there appears to be less and less migration from rural areas with the intention of remaining only a short time in the city and then returning to the village or the countryside. The probability of a rural migrant's staying for the remainder of his life in an urban setting appears to be increasing. If an individual comes to an urban area and stays away from the rural area for a period of ten or more years, he is extremely unlikely to return to the village except for occasional visits.[2]

Quantities and Characteristics

Who are the residents of urban areas? The numbers vary from country to country and according to the size of the cities. The statistics are overwhelming. Furthermore, dwellers in urban areas are found in great variations of living patterns, particularly with reference to density.

[1] J. Clyde Mitchell, "Urbanization, Detribalization, and Stabilization in Southern Africa: A Problem of Definition and Measurement," report of the International African Institute, London. Prepared under the auspices of UNESCO, *Social Implications of Industrialization and Urbanization in Africa South of the Sahara* (Paris: UNESCO, 1956), pp. 693–711 (hereafter referred to as UNESCO, *Africa South of the Sahara*).

[2] *Ibid.*, p. 703.

The Europeans or other Westerners who always have been small in numbers, proportionately speaking, have mostly lived in cities. There are some cases where Europeans in foreign countries have settled primarily on farms, as was true prior to independence in such countries as Kenya and South Africa. Usually, however, this has not been the typical pattern, and the European visitors—for this is in fact their status —have tended to settle in the urban areas where their accustomed comforts are likely to be accessible. The Europeans or Westerners have what Daryll Ford identifies as continuing association with external societies rather than primary responsibility and interest in the city where they may be living.[3] Moreover, they have attitudes and characteristics of resident transience in the urban area of a newly developing country. By and large, they see their assignments there as short-term in character and they seldom take on a long-term commitment to the urban area in which they find themselves. Primary interest at this point, however, is not in the proportionately small numbers of Europeans or Westerners who inhabit the cities of newly developing countries, but in the natives of these countries.

The summary of the characteristics of native urban residents in newly developing countries covers age, sex, education, occupation, income, morbidity and mortality, mental health, and fertility. Information about many of these subjects is relatively scarce and not uniformly available for all countries, so it will be necessary to make certain generalizations from which specific instances may depart somewhat.

An examination of the age of urban residents in newly developing countries reveals that there is a high proportion of the population in the age group 15 to 40. Often there will be a relatively small number of children proportional to the total population, although there are some exceptions to this as, for example, in the case of Hong Kong. Old people are also relatively few in number compared with their distribution in the country's total population, for most of the elder members of villages do not migrate cityward but tend to remain in the village. Also, the death rate being what it is in urban as well as rural areas of newly developing countries, there is not apt to be a large percentage of the population in the older age groups. This has been modified gradually in recent years by the startling advances in sanitation and medical care which have made possible a considerable lengthening of the life span. Some rather interesting implications of the small number of older people in the urban population have been suggested by S. Comhaire-Sylvain, who postulates that there may be a relationship between the small num-

[3] Daryll Ford, "Social Aspects of Urbanization and Industrialization in Africa: A General Review," in UNESCO, *Africa South of the Sahara,* pp. 48–49.

ber of older people in the urban population and the relative degree of stability in urban areas.[4] The evidence for this is not persuasive; however, if it is assumed that the presence of an older population affects the behavior of the younger population by virtue of respect and deference shown, then this might be of some relevance.

The characteristics of urban population as measured by differences in sex are variable from one part of the world to another. In economically developing countries of the West there is typically a larger proportion of females than males in urban areas. In newly developing countries, however, this same pattern may pertain, but there are many exceptions.[5]

In most newly developing countries, the urban areas have an excess of males over females. There is at least one notable exception in the case of Latin America. Judging from UNESCO reports, Latin America is characterized by a larger number of females than males in urban parts of its newly developing countries.[6] Perhaps this is affected somewhat by the stages of urbanization, long-established social customs, the employment of women outside the home, and various other differences between Latin American countries and developing countries elsewhere in the world.

With reference to urban educational levels, some entire countries have less than a score of college graduates. This is partly because of the relatively small number of persons who attended college, but it also results in some cases from attrition by nationals who were educated outside the country and have chosen not to return home. This obviously represents a very great net loss to the home country, since having a small percentage of the population college graduated results in a shortage of well-trained persons to conduct the evolution of the country into mature nationhood. In Latin America, however, it was found that illiteracy in urban areas was somewhat lower than expected.[7] Literacy generally is expected to be higher in urban than in rural areas and the evidence seems to indicate that is true for the urban areas of most newly developing countries.

The occupational characteristics of the urban population are interesting and serve as significant indicators of the relative attractiveness of life in such urban areas. Almost without exception the urban migrant comes to the city virtually totally unprepared to compete successfully —*i.e.*, above the day-laborer role—in the urban society. This is partly be-

[4] S. Comhaire-Sylvain, "Food and Leisure Among the African Youth of Leopoldville," in UNESCO, *Africa South of the Sahara*, p. 212.

[5] UN, *World Social Situation: 1957*, p. 118.

[6] UNESCO, *Latin America*, p. 28.

[7] UNESCO, *Latin America*, p. 64.

cause he lacks the skills, and sometimes even the language, as well as knowledge of the ways of the city by which he can introduce himself into the more productive aspects of the urban labor market. The multiplicity of urban occupational differences is increasing.

The marginally unemployable gravitate to the marginal services. There appear to be higher levels of employment in the services than in industrial occupations. This is quite in contrast to the West, where the service groups increase later in the urbanization process than apparently seems to be the case in newly developing countries.[8]

Most urban residents do not have an "occupation," but work wherever they can get a job. There are very great income differentials in the labor forces of developing countries. The ratio of professional to industrial workers' income, for example, may be 15 or 20 to 1, or even greater. This is in contrast to the West, where the difference between professional and industrial workers may be only 3 or 4 to 1. It is important to remember that in newly developing countries most of the workers are not engaged in industrial occupations. It is to be expected that there would be an even greater differential in income between professional and laborer occupations to which both male and female migrants, as well as residents of long duration, tend to gravitate.[9]

This distribution of the labor force in newly developing countries does not reflect any demonstrated incapacity of people to undertake urban occupations. It has been shown over and over again that even illiterates have the capacity to become employed in a machine technology. For example, the machine-tool makers observable in small-industry shops of many towns of India appear to develop much capacity to manufacture—by imitation—some of the high-grade Western machine tools! It is nevertheless true that ordinary urban residents are cut off from most of the higher-income supervisory, professional, semiprofessional, and managerial posts in the urban labor force and are almost exclusively restricted to the lower-income, day-to-day laborer category.

It is important to remember that the urban labor force in newly developing countries also includes fairly substantial numbers of children who must be counted as part of the labor force although, in general, they are only partially employed from time to time, and frequently gravitate toward the role of low-grade assistants or chore boys in some of the

[8] Wilbert E. Moore, *Social Change* (Englewood Cliffs, N.J.: Prentice-Hall, Inc., 1963), p. 101.

[9] R. B. Textor, *et al.*, *The Social Implications of Industrialization and Urbanization: Five Studies in Asia* (Calcutta: UNESCO Research Center on the Social Implications of Industrialization in Southern Asia, 1956), p. iv (hereafter referred to as Textor, ed., *Five Studies in Asia*).

other occupations. In addition, out of necessity to supplement the meager wages of their husbands, there are a substantial number of women in the labor market of many, but not all, countries. These women gravitate toward domestic types of service, although there may be great differentials from country to country as to the percentages of women in the total population who become involved even in this kind of activity.

As noted above, the wages earned by individual unskilled urban residents are extremely low and barely permit a subsistence kind of urbanization. The semiskilled fare somewhat better, but still do not even approach the levels observable in Western urbanization. Even the total family income is often not substantial enough to support the family with all its obligations on much more than a subsistence level.[10]

Sickness and death in newly developing countries are subjects about which not much detail is known. It is clear, however, that the medical facilities available in urban areas have had a substantial impact on the reduction of death rates, particularly in contrast to rural and remote areas where such medical facilities are not likely to exist. Mortality, in other words, is generally somewhat lower in urban areas than in rural areas. Data on length of life and its relationship to illness rates are very hard to secure; however, it is to be expected that the generally low nutritive diet and the very densely populated environment in which migrants, in particular, tend to live are not conducive to maintenance of a high level of health. In addition to their impact on the general health of urban populations, these conditions may, and frequently do, have a noticeable effect on even the mental health of the urban resident.[11]

ORIGINS OF THE URBAN POPULATION

If the plight of the urban resident is no more attractive than is suggested by the foregoing remarks, the question might well be raised as to why there is such a heavy migration to urban areas. Very little is known about the factors which impel residents of rural areas and villages to make their way into the large cities. There is a great deal of controversy as to whether they are "pushed" toward the urban areas because of circumstances over which they have no control, or whether the compelling reason for moving to urban areas is the "pull" which the urban area exerts over those who live elsewhere.

[10] N. D. Oram, "Aspects of Town Growth in Underdeveloped Countries," *Australian Planning Institute Journal,* **2** (April 1964), 274, citing UN, *World Social Situation: 1957,* p. 155.

[11] UN, *World Social Situation: 1957,* pp. 135–36.

"Push" versus "Pull" Factors

The "push" versus "pull" controversy is difficult to differentiate. It is quite clear that both push and pull factors have an impact upon the movement of rural and village populations into urban areas. The evidence seems to indicate that it is the push of existing rural circumstances which suggests to the rural resident that things might be better in the urban area.

Quite diverse factors affect migration to urban areas. If, for example, the land tenure system results in progressive fragmentation of land via multiple inheritance, or if the family structure is such that primogeniture causes younger sons to be displaced by the senior son who inherits all, then the capacity to survive either is reduced or virtually ceases to exist and additional candidates for migration—perhaps to urban areas—are the result.[12]

Among the factors which constitute the push that forces rural residents to migrate to urban areas must be included the following: overpopulation in rural areas, which has implications in terms of available food or work; too little opportunity for securing land that can be worked to produce a living; and reduced opportunities in government and business which may not expand at a rate required by the increase in rural population. The latter factor seems to exert the most push on rural residents to migrate to urban areas; however, this may not necessarily account for why rural migrants to the city stay there or why some of them return to the rural areas from which they originally came. The UNESCO publication *Urbanization in Asia and the Far East* suggests that the growth of cities is the result of such factors as "the low land-population ratio arising from the rapid population growth in relation to agricultural resources" as well as "the disruption and disorganization produced by the last war and political changes which followed."[13]

In addition, the seasonal nature of employment in agriculture normally involves a period between the planting of crops and their harvesting that automatically provides an opportunity, when there is not much work elsewhere, for possible migration to the urban area.

There may be a sense of relative deprivation which arises in rural areas once the inhabitants recognize that there are other, notably urban, places where they might live, presumably where living standards are higher than they are accustomed to in the country. Rural residents learn to want more of what the city has and they view with great interest

[12] The author is indebted to Neil Smelser for the reminder that these are also "push" factors that condition migration rates.

[13] UNESCO, *Asia and the Far East,* p. 34.

the reported higher income, access to education, and other rumored facilities of the urban area. They also view with great interest the wider freedoms from restraints that are reported to exist in urban areas, irrespective of the fact that these expectations may be only false hopes.

Some rural residents have been exposed to urban lure by military service or civil disturbances in the countryside, especially, for example, in connection with World War II and the following years. Any invasion and lack of security in a rural area ordinarily has the consequence of pushing whatever population can move toward the city. Revolutions such as in the partition of India and Pakistan produce refugees who gravitate mostly toward the great cities.

The lure or pull of the great city is generated partly from experiences such as these and partly by the "feedback" about the benefits, or at least the claimed benefits, of life in the city, irrespective of their degree of attainability. Better roads, radio, government representatives moving through the countryside, and similar communication influences have much to do with the nature and quality of the feedback to rural areas from the city, and the differential sorting out of claimed advantages and disadvantages.

There even may be elements of national policy involved in the movement of population from rural to urban areas. The collectivization of agriculture in some cases creates a labor surplus in rural areas, impelling people to move to urban areas. The allocation of national funds to industrial development in the major cities, in preference to the investment of such funds in rural areas, may make the city look much more attractive than the rural area to the discriminating rural dweller.

Donald J. Bogue and K. C. Zachariah come to the conclusion, with reference to characteristics of urban migrants, that:

1. Rural-to-urban migration in India is not negligible, but is a very widespread phenomenon.

2. Streams of migration are flowing not only toward the very largest cities, but also to hundreds of medium-size and smaller cities in all regions, except those adversely affected by partition.

3. Although originally this migration may have some of the aspects of a "pioneering" movement, comprised predominantly of males, the 1941–1951 decade witnessed the removal to the cities of almost as many women as men.

4. There is little evidence of reluctance on the part of the villagers to seek their fortunes in the city. In fact, the unemployment data suggest that they crowd into the cities seeking work. Very possibly, unemployment in the cities, rather than the restrictive effect of cultural tradition in the villages, is the major brake upon rural-to-urban migration at the present time.

5. This upswing in urbanward migration probably is a fairly recent phe-

nomenon which began in the late 1930's. It has now progressed to a point where the residents of almost every village have relatives or fellow villagers living in at least one (and possibly several) of the major cities. Family and village ties are sufficiently strong to create an obligation upon the successful migrant to help sponsor new entrants to the city. With villagers becoming progressively more oriented toward the new urbanized economy, and with migration channels firmly established, the nation seems to be all set to enter a phase of unprecedented urbanization, assisted by the prevailing family system and culture rather than hindered by it.[14]

Although these data pertain to India, it appears from other information that they are not at all atypical; in fact they are characteristic of the kinds of migration taking place elsewhere in newly developing countries.

In reviewing the migration of rural inhabitants into urban areas in newly developing countries, it is interesting to observe that, beginning with the colonial period in southeast Asia, the Middle East, the Indian subcontinent, and Latin America, a kind of tropism developed in the attraction of rural population to the great city.

Origin by International Migration

It was not only the rural population that was caught up in migration from one place to another and particularly toward urban areas. There have also been international migrations to and among urban areas, such as the movement of rather large numbers of Indians from their homeland to various ports in southeast Asia and to Hong Kong, the migration of Indians to South Africa, and the migration of Chinese into Hong Kong, Rangoon, and Bangkok. More recently international migrations have been sparked by the partition of India and Pakistan and the establishment of the state of Israel, taking quite different kinds of migration to urban areas in newly developing countries. The tropism, however, has primarily affected the rural population living in areas near cities. While migrations on an international scale have often involved considerable distances, the majority of intra-country migrations appear to be relatively short-distance moves.

"Laws" of Migration to Cities

It would be helpful for predictive purposes to be able to refer with confidence to "laws" of migration to urban areas in newly developing

[14] Donald J. Bogue and K. C. Zachariah, "Urbanization and Migration in India," in Roy Turner, ed., *India's Urban Future* (Berkeley and Los Angeles, Calif.: University of California Press, 1962), p. 45.

countries. The fact is that very little is presently known about these migration patterns, although studies in process may reveal a much higher level of information than has been available. There is some evidence, for example, to suggest that migration occurs first from rural or village areas to small towns and then to bigger and bigger towns. However, there is also considerable evidence that this step-by-step migration may not take place, but rather that rural migrants move first to small cities and then to big ones—as may be observed in the case of Brazil.[15] This has been disputed by Harley L. Browning, who believes that migration does not proceed in this step fashion. If there are any laws of migration to urban areas they are likely to vary somewhat from country to country, depending upon the circumstances. For example, the sizable influx of migrants to certain mining centers in South Africa involves a complex set of relationships and patterns of modern migration which might not be characteristic of other countries where migration takes place so heavily for purposes of working in extractive industries. There is evidence of seasonal, reverse, and multiple migration, further discussed below.

It appears also that there is a certain amount of "floating migration," composed of people who wander from one city to another, desperately trying to make a place for themselves. M. B. Deshmukh noted in his Delhi study: "No less than 65 per cent [of the migrants] had tried their luck first in from 6 to 15 other towns or even more."[16]

Selectivity in Migration

A related question of interest is that of selectivity. Who moves into urban areas? Again, the evidence is inconclusive. A great many observations made on this particular point rest not on detailed assembly of data but careful observation of particular cases. There does seem to be evidence that there is a selectivity by sex, that males, for example, tend to be much more mobile in that they move from country to city in Asian and African countries. As already noted, however, in Latin America there is evidence that women predominate slightly in the movement from rural to urban areas.[17] This is true in all cases, apparently, except in that of Andean Indians where males predominate. There has been much speculation to explain these continental differences. It has been

[15] UN, *World Social Situation: 1957*, p. 175. See also Harley L. Browning, "Recent Trends in Latin American Urbanization," *Annals of the American Academy of Political and Social Science*, **316** (March 1958), 111–20.

[16] M. B. Deshmukh, "A Study of Floating Migration," in UNESCO, *Africa South of the Sahara*, pp. ix, 143ff.

[17] UNESCO, *Latin America*, pp. 100ff.

suggested, for example, that possibly the urbanization in Latin America is more advanced, so that there is a differential decrease in the percentage of males moving to urban areas, a closer approximation to Western experience in general.

Differential or selective migration by education of migrants is an intriguing subject. Although the evidence is very limited, it appears that in India, for example, the more highly educated move in larger numbers.[18] Other studies have also presented similar data. It bears repeating, however, that the evidence on this point is quite inconclusive. If taken from another point of view, it might be implied, as one author indicated, that perhaps it is the rural "misfits" who find themselves incompatible with rural society and therefore are impelled to move to the urban area.[19] Obviously, the use of the word "misfit" does not necessarily imply any inferior intelligence; rather, misfit refers to individuals who seek a different climate in which to explore the potentialities of their own personalities and capacities. There is evidence to suggest that, in any case, the movement from rural to urban areas takes place irrespective of any demonstrated demand for the labor of those who make the move.

Many fascinating questions remain unanswered. For example, is there anything to suggest that at the present time there is a wider range of rural types migrating to cities than was formerly the case? Are there any differentials in status, age, and roles of persons now moving to urban areas as compared with those in earlier periods?

INTERNAL AND TEMPORAL VARIATIONS IN MIGRATION

Little is known about internal and temporal changes in the characteristics of recent, as compared with past, migration to urban areas. There are very few data on the distance from which people migrate to the city. There is some knowledge about physical mobility of migrants within urban areas as, for example, in Delhi, where urban migrants must follow construction jobs, or in Baghdad, where workers may move to be as close as possible to other kinds of employment. There is, of course, the mandatory mobility involved in forced moves when squatter areas are cleared by local administrative action and new living places, no matter how temporary, have to be found.

[18] Bogue and Zachariah, *op. cit.*, pp. 51ff.

[19] Wilbert E. Moore, "Industrialization and Social Change," in B. F. Hoselitz and W. E. Moore, eds., *Industrialization and Society* (Paris and The Hague: UNESCO-Mouton, 1963), pp. 332–33.

Mobility

Considerable importance is attached to seasonal and other types of variations in mobility, such as reverse migration and cyclical trends. In many parts of the world a long period between the planting of crops and their harvesting provides an interval during which temporary migration to urban areas is potentially possible. This is a period during which women are left responsible for minimal care of the fields, and the head of the family returns to the village for the harvest. Some migration—particularly the first migration to an urban area—may very well take place under these circumstances.

Seasonal and Other Variations

There are other kinds of temporary migration, ranging from a few weeks to several months or even years in the case of young men who migrate under contract to spend a limited, predesignated period of time in the employment of a mining company. Ordinarily this does not involve taking along their families; rather, it is a solitary move by individuals who are temporarily housed at company expense, fulfill their contract, and then return to their villages or rural areas. More often, however, people migrate for a relatively short period of time to begin with, and then on a second or succeeding migration are more likely to stay. With each trip they learn more about coping with their urban experiences; therefore, each successive exposure to the city makes it easier for them to remain and less attractive for them to return to their rural areas.

The question of reverse migration—that is, the back-to-the-village migration—of former residents is one of great interest. With the exception of cases where it is customary for one to migrate for a short period, save a small sum of money, and then return to the village, the evidence seems to indicate that there is very little reverse migration. Several factors may be at work here. In some cases it is a matter of pride; in the effort to preserve face, a person who has not succeeded in an urban area is not likely to go back to a village. Moreover, the capacity to represent oneself as being successful tends to affect the differential feedback of information from urban to rural area, with only the "good news" going back to the village. J. Clyde Mitchell suggests that if a rural migrant stays away from his rural area for a period of ten or more years, except for occasional holiday visits, it is extremely unlikely that he will ever return to live there.[20] Mitchell has created an index of stabilization

[20] Mitchell, *loc. cit.*

of urbanization which calculates the probabilities of this phenomenon. In addition, there is some evidence that rural-to-urban migration is more nearly permanent in Latin America than in some newly developing countries elsewhere.[21] S. N. Agarwala adduces evidence that, as might be expected, in older age groups the reverse migration is higher than in the younger age groups.[22]

THE URBAN INDIVIDUAL AND THE FAMILY

In viewing urban inhabitants, their lives, and society it must be remembered that migrants descend upon the city from some other place with its own highly developed culture, much of which these migrants carry to the city no matter how intensely they may attempt to reject it. These migrants are not ciphers, not fully pliable clay; they come to the urban area with an overlay of rural tribal tradition and established ways of doing things, loyalty and obligation patterns, economic arrangements, and systems of constraints in channels of communication which do not readily die in the urban context. In fact, these customs are strongly supported by the kind of environment into which a migrant is likely to move.

The Urban Individual

Thus the migrant's posture in the new urban context involves responses to his old culture, conflicts and tensions with the new—and usually quite different—urban context and the new roles. Not only must he survive physically, the migrant must also survive in the largely alien socioeconomic context. It is impossible for him lightly to detach himself from his background. He is provided with few criteria to decide what parts of the new culture to embrace and what to reject, what he should refashion and rationalize as the new way, and what of his past life and practices he should push into the background or preserve. It is not easy to substitute, for example, a pecuniary nexus for that of the village bush variety of obligations. The strains come partly from the necessary rate of change from rural to urban ways of life, a kind of compulsive convertibility on which a high price is laid. As will be shown, sometimes this compulsive convertibility for survival purposes

[21] Philip M. Hauser, "Rapporteurs' Report," in UNESCO, *Latin America,* p. 45.

[22] S. N. Agarwala, "A Method for Estimating Decade Internal Migration in Cities in India from Indian Census Data," *Indian Economic Review,* 4, No. 1 (February 1958), 71.

has rather negative or even antisocial results, there being some evidence, for example, that the related tension and strain are associated with higher rates of alcoholism, drug addiction, juvenile delinquency, crime, and mental disorders.[23]

Mere physical presence in an urban area does not necessarily have implications for an individual's participation in urban life. A migrant may very well be *in* a city but not *of* that city—that is, actually involved socially. The universe of contacts of a migrant may be extremely limited, especially in the early stages of his residence in the urban area. This arises partly because of his unfamiliarity with the urban way of life. Furthermore his experience—or lack of it—his dress, language, and his customs may effectively cut him off from most of the urban society into which he moves. His tendency to seek out his "own kind" in the urban area still further restricts him. This may lead to partly self-imposed segregation that derives from the fact that many people around him have come from different tribes, different geographic areas, or different cultures of which he is innately suspicious. Sometimes the residential sorting out and clustering of people from diverse origins leads to the emergence of "quarters" or settlements populated entirely or almost entirely by people from a particular district, tribe, or tradition. The in-feeling of these settlements may become so great, because of the frustration of dealing with the outside society, that they may even develop their own unofficial government, courts, and other specialized and origin-related institutions.

Nevertheless, resocialization of the rural migrant is required for adaptation to what is essentially a new way of life. This will generally proceed differentially in terms of rate of change of specific urban practices. The migrant may, for instance, accept modern pecuniary relationships but retain the use of tribal medicine men. Conflicts between and among these differences in the acceptability of urban practices and customs may lead to strains, discontinuities, and conflicts for the migrant. A member of a rural society can be expected to exhibit differential acceptability of the practices and customs with which he is surrounded; the pressures for accepting prevailing practices in rural areas usually result in unquestioning compliance, but in an urban area virtually everything may appear strange to the new migrant and lead to retention of selected rural customs.

The individual in an urban area, free from the village and tribal restraints to which he has been subjected, may, however, gravitate toward

[23] Moore, *op. cit.*, p. 343; and Ford, *op. cit.*, pp. 36, 42, 43, 46ff.

his own kind—that is, his own tribe or geographic settlement group—and therefore may remain under duress of survival necessity. For example, in the case of India, if the migrant gravitates toward his village group, his caste is likely to be known; therefore, any attempt to "pass" into a different caste status may be very much restricted. His role-jumping capacity or potential is thereby affected. Nevertheless, it is the sense of anomie—*i.e.*, normlessness—and of being "lost" in the urban society that drives large numbers of single, unattached persons migrating from the village to associate themselves with former village residents possessing a longer experience with the urban society.

The rural migrant to the city may appear to have a great opportunity to escape the social or caste stratification characteristic of his village origin. It often happens, however, that the familiar rural stratification is replaced by urban stratification. In fact, the village resident moving into the city often finds himself in the midst of a situation where industrialization and urbanization have produced a context having a greater —*i.e.*, more complex—stratification than that from which he came.

The Urban Family

As always, family is one of the most significant institutions in urban areas of newly developing countries. To understand the family in such a context it is important, first, to call attention to some of the more nearly common characteristics. It is very likely that, by leaving the village or his rural surroundings, the migrant to an urban area has moved from an environment in which he had a very close affiliation with a family group. If he has first encountered the city alone, he will find himself in a comparatively strange context. If he has arrived with his family group, he will still find that the urban environment exerts rather impressive influences on the family and brings about subtle changes. The necessity to adapt to different contexts in the urban area, the residence-crowding the family finds in the urban environment, and the exposure to a new urban way of doing things inevitably have some effect on the family as an institution. In general, these influences accelerate departures from the old ways of life. For example, the family member may find himself under increasing pressures to develop new kinds of obligations that he previously did not have in the village; these obligations will have an impact on the family and kinship obligation patterns to which he was formerly accustomed.

In the city the migrant is exposed to a continual erosion of family control over its individual members. This is particularly pronounced if an individual has come to the city by himself and is not part of a family group. But even where the total family or a large portion of it has migrated together to the urban area, the individual becomes involved in circumstances that gradually force him to assume a new family role. He may out of necessity work at a distance from other members of the family; he may develop new contacts which affect and limit the contacts he is able to maintain with his family members.

Traditional patterns may have to give way under the new environment. For example, the usual arrangements for establishing a husband and wife relationship may be greatly modified in the new urban context, one result being that instead of proceeding with the normal rituals and practices associated with mate selection, the individual—particularly if he has come to the city independently of his family—may find himself participating in a series of informal relationships with members of the opposite sex that do not exhibit the normal marriage relationship to which he was earlier exposed, but are a series of cohabitations. In effect, by doing so the individual not only modifies the rural customs with which he is familiar, but may involve himself in a series of sexual alliances that may place severe strains on his old mores.

Women in particular tend to find their position, their roles, and their activities intensively modified by the urban environment. The legal and economic changes in their relationships with other members of their family are most pronounced.[24] A wife may find that different legal provisions affecting women in urban areas have a rather important impact on her legal status; for example, she may be able to hold real estate in her own name. Furthermore, whereas in the village wives and children were considered economic assets because of their ability to work in the fields, in the city they may be considered economic liabilities because of the cost of supporting them. On the other hand, women may find themselves involved in a subtle, if not apparent, shift in the relationships they have with their husbands. Experience seems to indicate, for example, a likelihood of an increase in the conjugal type of relationship to their husbands, rather than a merely convenient arrangement induced by the system of arranging marriages in village areas. The kinds of responsibilities and obligations to their husbands may be substantially altered.

The urban family will also find its hospitality obligations somewhat modified from the rural origin patterns. It is customary, for example, for urban families to offer hospitality to any member of a related village

[24] Meran McCulloch, "Survey of Recent and Current Field Studies on the Social Effects of Economic Development in Inter-Tropical Africa," in UNESCO, *Africa South of the Sahara*, pp. 216–19.

family who has newly come to the city and is seeking to make his way there. It is expected that the relatives who have preceded him to the city will find a place for him in the family circle, or at least provide food and lodging on a temporary or even long-term basis until the individual can establish himself. Such compulsive hospitality has no legal limits, with the result that a new arrival from a rural area to the city may expect to be accepted in this system for even rather extended periods of time. In some respects this hospitality obligation is not new to the former village resident who has been accustomed to share responsibilities for members of the village. On the other hand, it may involve a relationship which is absolutely necessary for survival in the urban area. The family income of the urban residents may be so low that it is absolutely essential to supplement this income by whatever small contributions can be made by the recently arrived rural migrant to the city. This equivalent of taking in roomers or boarders, either with or without compensation, is a difficult undertaking in an urban context where living conditions are generally such that there is barely room for the family itself, let alone additional residents.

Because of the economic advantages involved, it is quite common for a family to take in strangers as boarders or roomers who will share the fate of the family itself. These persons may not even have migrated from the same area or the same village, thereby introducing potential conflicts due to differences in background, dietary practices, and so on.

Observers of family life in urban areas of newly developing countries customarily have deplored the impact of the urban environment upon traditional family arrangements. Generally they have claimed that there is an almost inevitable deterioration in the family under urban conditions, particularly in comparison with rural family arrangements. There is some evidence, however, to indicate that the transfer of family life from rural to urban areas does not necessarily lead to breakdown.[25]

There does seem to be some agreement that it is the child who is most likely to receive the greatest impact as a result of disruptions of family life. This results partly from having to live in an environment inimical to the development of a happy childhood and a strong family relationship, but primarily it appears to be related to the fact that both father and mother may find it necessary to be absent from the home during the day in order to earn enough money to support the family. This automatically leaves the child without supervision and care; also it frequently places upon him a compulsion to find ways of earning money that can be used to supplement the family income.[26]

[25] UN, *World Social Situation: 1957,* pp. 137ff.
[26] *Ibid.,* p. 139.

CLASS STRUCTURE AND GROUP AFFILIATION

The development of social classes among native urban residents appears to vary greatly among newly developing countries. There are numerous factors which may affect the extent to which stratification and class development take place. For example, Meran McCulloch, in summarizing a series of studies on Africa south of the Sahara, mentions certain factors which hinder the development of social classes in urban areas.[27] Attention is called to the fact that the residence of a class in a separate area is not practicable. Furthermore, family responsibilities and obligations placed upon more successful urban residents with reference to new migrants coming into the city are such that there is likely to be a breakdown because of whatever differences there might be between new migrants and older, more successful ones. These migrants are placed in an obligation relationship to one another which imputes a level of equal importance. Another factor referred to in McCulloch's summary is mentioned by M. Parker with reference to education which, if it is successful and on a high level, might bring about demands for facilities beyond the income of the person involved. An individual, therefore, may associate himself with one class culturally but be limited to another class economically. It is also noted that women are likely to be more loyal and oriented to tribal customs than men, making it difficult for their husbands to move from one class status to another. McCulloch also refers to another factor noted by Parker, namely, the slowness of economic differentiation in the non-Western population of urban areas in newly developing countries. This inevitably affects the capacity of individuals to exhibit the externally noticeable possessions and other criteria which in turn may affect the movement from one class to another. McCulloch further summarizes many of the studies, referring to the "cleavage between Europeans and Africans [which] overshadows economic differences within the African community itself." This circumstance is not unique to Africa. One of the complicating aspects of changes in class and caste differences or status in urban areas is the temporary, if not long-lasting, persistence of old and new status differentials.

Class stratification may vary somewhat with the size and age of the city, the length of the residence of the migrants, and so on. It appears

[27] McCulloch, *op. cit.*, pp. 215ff. See also position of M. Parker, pp. 127ff. Typical studies of urban society in various parts of Africa and elsewhere have been prepared by the following: Leo Kuper, Michael Banton, Arthur T. Porter, Ione Acquah, Philip Mayer, Hilston Watts, Ronald Davies, A. W. Southall and P. C. W. Gutkind, Barrington Kaye, and Theodore Caplow.

that there is less class differentiation in west coast African and central African cities than in Egypt and some other African cities of the Mediterranean.

Group affiliation and organization in urban areas of newly developing countries must be discussed in the context of the fact that in the rural area the family tends to control most of the life of the individual. That is, the relationships a member bears to his family predominate during his entire life. Conversely, in the city it is quite early evident that group identification progressively controls more and more segments of a person's life and is largely a substitute for the rural type of family control.

By seeking out his village predecessors and depending upon them heavily for introduction to the urban society, the migrant may expose himself to a situation in which the earlier migrating village predecessors come to exercise substantial control over his welfare. They may communicate only selected aspects of information that the new migrant may require, leaving the already established migrants in a position to obtain the more favorable opportunities. In some cases this basically heavy dependence upon his predecessors is extreme, as in the situation of the Bantu migrant to the South African city who, if he speaks with a "click," may not be able to communicate readily with those who do not. Under such circumstances it may be that he can make his way only by associating with a larger and older group. This is not a situation limited to newly developing countries: the southern white mountaineer migrant to Chicago, for example, may find himself most readily acceptable to his former associates who have migrated to Chicago and use the same archaic language.

The tendency to affiliate and remain affiliated with origin groups is likely to involve a transplant of rural culture into the urban context, producing a private "cocoon" society inside another society, perhaps partly for protective purposes in insulating migrants against the culture conflicts and stresses of the new environment. It should also be noted that not all of the individuals who migrate to a particular urban area will have come from the same place of origin, either in terms of tribe or geographic area. The same urban area may be populated by tribals from different—and sometimes even warring or hostile—groups who cannot be expected to forget all these distinctions just because they have moved into an urban area. This transfer of animosities to the urban context may be still another reason why the migrant may tend to associate himself with predecessors from his own group.

There may emerge a kind of "super-tribalization" of the sort referred to by Jean Rouch as taking place in Kumasi and Accra. Daryll Ford also refers to "the [native] military tradition [which] was rephrased in terms of the conquest of market sites and monopolies of occupations and lines of trade" in some of the situations he analyzed with reference to tribal affiliations of migrants to urban areas.[28]

It is not only the old tribal predecessor to whom the new migrant is attracted. The urban context itself presents new avenues and opportunities for new types of association. Many are attracted to participation in a union, politics on a very modest level, credit or loan groups, and similar organizations. There is a great range in the degree of association. The most informal groupings may at once be both the most satisfying and the most accessible to newcomers in the city. They may not necessarily be organized in the sense of having constitutions, dues, rules, and regulations, but they may be very effective in terms of either temporary or permanent mutual aid organizations. The very lack of sophistication and identification with power media drives the migrant into mutual assistance groups and associations. As Richard M. Morse has said:

> The hiatus between urban bureaucratic structures and the agrarian background of the migrant is so great that accommodation of one to the other can be expected only after the migrants have grouped themselves, if possible with understanding guidance, in *ad hoc* transitional associations.[29]

URBAN INSTITUTIONS IN NEWLY DEVELOPING COUNTRIES

The institutional patterning that takes place in urban areas of newly developing countries may perhaps best be discussed by reference to specific institutional patterns. Not all of these will be considered here but special attention, for illustrative purposes, will be devoted to religion, education, and government. Throughout the discussion it should be understood that institutional changes referred to may not be exclusively the result of urbanization but are also influenced by industrialization, bureaucratization, and other concomitant features of modernization.

Religion

The relationship of an urban resident to his religion will vary according to whether his religious practice involves private or group action. In the case of southeast Asia, for example, Hindu or Buddhist devotions

[28] Daryll Ford, "Introductory Survey," in UNESCO, *Africa South of the Sahara,* pp. 38–39.

[29] "Latin American Cities: Aspects of Function and Structure," reprinted in J. Friedmann and William Alonso, eds., *Regional Planning and Development: A Reader* (Cambridge, Mass.: Massachusetts Institute of Technology Press, 1964), p. 378, originally published in *Comparative Studies on Society and History,* 4 (July 1962).

may be exercised primarily on a private basis either in or out of a sanctuary. In such cases the religious shrine or sanctuary may be the single most nearly stable focus in an urban resident's life. In Moslem cities the mosque may provide not only a place of worship, but also the only place of real quiet, the only place where open space may be available in which to sit and not be quite so pressed by hordes of people. The urban resident who practices his religion by private or independent worship is likely to find a multitude of convenient wayside and other sanctuaries. A Moslem will find that the practice of religion in urban areas is not substantially different from that in rural areas since it is mostly a private affair, though he may also choose to associate himself with a larger group in the mosque.

Where the practice of religion is much more related to group participation, as in the case of West African cities, opportunities for such religious observance may not be as great as they were in the countryside. This often provides an occasion for the migrant to return to his village for communal ceremonial occasions. Some of the religious and group customs are relatively unworkable in the urban area. A city is hardly the place for pursuing the Transkei (South Africa) ritual in which a young initiate must go 30 days in the wilderness on his own with only a stick and a skin for cover before he can be accepted into the society.

Even though religious practices and other related activities may have rural origins, many of these survive the transfer into urban areas. The survival of witchcraft, for example, as illustrated in the markets of Kano and Ibadan where one can buy requisite animal skins, feathers, entrails, bones, and parts of animal anatomy for the concoction of remedies or potions, suggests that not all of the rural practice is dropped when the individual moves to an urban area.

Secularization, nevertheless, makes undeniable inroads on religion. The old forms may survive but more likely new forms and practices emerge. The urban resident may be unable to practice the customs to which he had been related previously, or the inconvenience involved may also help invoke additional strains and tensions between the old practice and the new, the old context and the new.

Education

Education in the urban area is often characterized by a shortage of teachers, buildings, books, and other facilities. There is a particular need for vocational training facilities which, by and large, tend not to be provided in the urban context. This is most crucial because of the necessity of the agricultural worker to convert himself into an individual who can apply his native skills to new industrial and other urban types of occupations.

Even in cases where urban educational facilities exist in limited numbers, they are likely to be more readily available to the established residents than to the new ones. The new migrant also may not be qualified by residence or acquaintance with the procedures by which he can take advantage of whatever educational facilities exist.

There is a related anomaly to this gross undereducation of the total urban population in a tendency toward an oversupply of university-educated unemployables. Smaller newly developing countries are usually not bothered by this problem, but larger countries, such as India, may find themselves in a position where they have an excess of university-trained people who, because of the present state of the development of the economy and the government, do not have an opportunity to apply their skills in middle-range positions. A university graduate in India may find it necessary to move from city to city, living with relative after relative in a desperate effort to locate a position in which he can use his university training. This is a situation which will be compensated for over time, but at present in India there is an oversupply of university-trained people relative to the opportunities available in the Indian society.

In sharp contrast are those smaller newly developing countries with a gross undersupply of university-trained people; they are thereby understaffed in industry, government, and trade. This underemployment or unemployment of university-trained people may adversely affect the efficiency with which the governmental bureaucracy and business organizations are able to act. The oversupply phenomenon is partly due to the failure—up to now—of countries to develop middle-range positions, but also partly due to the failure of universities to train appropriately the persons who are required to staff those positions. Where there is underemployment, the situation reflects not so much the shortage of trained people as the shortage of appropriately trained people.

Government

Governmental institutions are of particular interest in urban areas of newly developing countries. In general, newly developing countries have no prevailing tradition of public—*i.e.*, broad-based—participation in the governmental process. In tribal rule, for example, authority comes from the hereditary chiefs and this is generally unquestioned. Administration from "outside" during colonialism was also a kind of governmental arrangement that did not brook much participation by the general public.

Furthermore, former rural migrants—who compose most of the urban population—are unfamiliar with urban governmental forms. This unfamiliarity with urban governmental forms together with a carry-over of tribal ways of doing things into the urban environment greatly reduces the potential for public participation in urban government.

The urban government itself is exposed to some serious strains. Generally much larger demands for services are placed upon it than it can provide. Also, there are hordes of migrants from different tribes—not all of which are compatible—that have to be supervised and ordered in such a way as to prevent internal difficulties for the city. Furthermore, the relative deprivation in which most of the urban population finds itself always carries with it threats from new leaders among the discontented, pressures from "have-not's" who no longer retain the high level of aspiration they brought from rural areas. Not only are there demands from the general public, but new powers in the urban community such as industrialists exert pressures for their own benefits. Urban government in newly developing countries is generally underfinanced and cannot cope with the scale of problems with which it is confronted. The situation is a vicious circle, for lack of capacity—in terms of finance, equipment, and direction—to cope with the sanitation problem, for example, is likely to produce situations in which the disease level is increased which, in turn, creates more government responsibilities for medical care. The great mass of the urban population does not have the capacity to provide tax returns to the municipal government of such a dimension that it can cope effectively with such tasks as the provision of a sewage system. There appears to be an inevitable, and almost invariably increasing, gap between resources available to metropolitan administrations and the demands placed upon them.

Under such circumstances it sometimes is a temptation for the municipalities—especially those housing a national government headquarters—to indulge in other kinds of expenditures which may appear to be very inconsistent with unmet needs. For example, funds may be allocated in what appears to be a lavish way for the erection of public prestige buildings, perhaps reflecting some feeling that these may help symbolize the emergence of these newly developing countries. Presidential palaces, skyscraper office buildings, and similar structures relevant to the needs of only a very small percentage of the population may be preferred to investment in municipal sewage systems. Bypassing of the requirements of the urban millions in favor of impressing countrymen or the outside world by prestige buildings is only one of the major difficulties involved in coping with urban problems.

In general, the great masses of the urban population seem able to exert very little impact on solving their plight. There may be no readily available channels for them to express their complaints. Moreover, there sometimes exists a mutual suspicion between residents and political leaders. This suspicion may arise partly from an incapacity to communicate, literally, with reference to goals; or it may just reflect a lack of experience in providing means for residents to affect urban decision-making in the future. Feelings of unbridgeable distance and lurking distrust between the ordinary resident and the bureaucracy, gaps in communication, gulfs between promises and performance in amelioration of problems, and the inability of the urban resident to find a "handle" by which he can alter his lot may turn him toward the kinds of voluntary associations referred to earlier. At the least, these organizations may cope with any simple needs such as insuring one against heavy costs associated with funerals, weddings, other special celebrations, and similar personal crises.

The general job insecurity of the ordinary urban resident is such that although he may have a rather ambiguous view toward his government, he nevertheless regards employment by the government as one of the surest routes to security. Many urban residents, therefore, exhibit a strong desire and effort to use whatever avenues are available, including family affiliation and tribal responsibilities from one group to another, to secure a post in the government occupational structure.

The government must necessarily stand in an ambivalent relationship to its clientele, the urban residents. As Lucian W. Pye has noted:

> To bring large numbers of people into urban life always means inducting them into some form of politics . . . [will it be constructive or anti-social?]. If this process can be carried out without alienation and damaging consequences the polity can rapidly gain in benefits of an enlarged citizenry; but if the process is marred by tension and conflict, permanent scars can be left on the polity and become a continuous source of trouble for the effective operation of the political process.[30]

Urban governments in rapidly developing countries have not completely solved the problem of how to induct their populations into the governing process without encountering corresponding dangers.

[30] Lucian W. Pye, "The Political Implications of Urbanization and the Development Process," in *United Nations Conference on the Application of Science and Technology for the Benefit of the Less Developed Areas, Geneva, 1963, United States Papers* (Washington, D.C.: U.S. Government Printing Office, 1962), p. 89. In the same paper Pye also noted: "If lonely people come to the cities in search of a better existence and cannot even find the satisfactions of employment, they are likely in time to turn to increasingly antisocial activities in order to find a sense of belonging and becoming again a member of a community" (p. 85).

GENERAL CONSIDERATIONS

Perhaps a summary picture of the inhabitant of urban areas in newly developing countries may be suggested by the following:

> Many cities in Asia and the Far East, in contrast with Western cities, often retain strong village characteristics or those of an agglomeration of villages. In general they tend to be characterized by the coexistence of two distinctive areas: (1) the Western type area, and (2) the indigenous type area consisting of an agglomeration of villages. In consequence, although a rather small elite indigenous population appears in Asian cities with the same characteristics as those possessed by urban residents in the West, the mass population of many Asian cities are resident in village agglomerations and tend to retain "folk" characteristics. The characteristics of the urban resident, identified with such dichotomies of continua as the "folk-urban," "rural-urban," or "community-society" categories, do not hold for the mass of residents in many Asian cities.[31]

All that needs to be changed in the above selection to make it applicable to cities in other developing countries is the geographic reference!

Rural Transplants

The phenomenon of "rural transplants" or survivals in urban areas is a common one. Indeed, it may be these rural transplants or survivals of rural practices who insulate the new migrant against his new environment until he can become accustomed to it. As a result, there may not be nearly as much cultural shock involved in the move from a rural to an urban area as may at one time have been thought. The cultural shock is related to the change from a subsistence economy to a cash economy, from the caste role or a class status to employment dealing with machines and the corresponding shifts in status as a result of funds earned, or sometimes from high-status rural laborer to low-status urban laborer. All of these may induce a kind of malaise or apathy deriving from the frustrations involved.[32]

Cultural conflicts are inevitable. In Rangoon, for example, in front of each house a little abode is erected for the guardian spirit of that house to dwell in. Continuing this rural custom in the city is not difficult if it is possible to identify each separate residence. But suppose several

[31] UNESCO, *Asia and the Far East,* pp. 34–35.

[32] G. Malengreau, "Observations on the Orientation of Sociological Researches in African Urban Centers, with Reference to the Situation in the Belgian Congo," in UNESCO, *Africa South of the Sahara,* pp. 624–38; and Ford, *op. cit.,* p. 46.

hundred families, involving perhaps a dozen different guardian spirits, live in one government housing project. Which spirit is chosen to protect the structure? Which spirit dwells in the spirit house?

There may be a strange mixture of new and surviving concepts in the urban family of a newly developing country. Some notions may be carried over from the rural context, such as the pattern of worship. On the other hand, new relationships may quite readily emerge. Take, for example, the question of family authority. Does the male head of the household lose his status if only his wife is able to find a job and thus supports the family? Or what is the influence of caste and tribal authority if the new urban migrant avoids association with earlier migrants from his village? The whole course of a migrant's life may be changed by his decision with reference to that question. This is particularly significant in view of the fact that, in reality, seldom does a migrant decide not to affiliate himself with his predecessors in the urban area.

Expectation versus Achievement

As noted, one of the unique aspects of life in urban society is the coexistence of old and new status systems, the legacy of rural status systems coexisting with the new urban-induced variety. The opportunity of a particular individual for achievement consonant with his aspirations is often hopelessly remote; the probability that success will be achieved is low. There is a limit even to the number of rickshaws to be pushed, pulled, or peddled; rural skills are only moderately marketable in the big city. Almost invariably there is a labor force surplus in those categories for which the newcomer qualifies. There tends to be, therefore, a vast gulf between an individual's capacity and opportunity for achieving his aspirations in the city.

Alternatives to Subsistence Urbanization

Perhaps the most overwhelming phenomenon of all the characteristics of urban inhabitants is the subsistence urbanization level of living to which they are exposed, and from which they are quite unlikely to escape even after a long period of life in the city. The grossly low level of subsistence urbanization may be so close to an agricultural subsistence level of living that the difference may be just one of locale. This plight may be even more intolerable when it is daily compared with examples of the opposite extreme in level of living enjoyed by a lucky few.

One alternative to this urban subsistence condition is to stay on the land or in the village, an alternative which is generally unacceptable to an individual once he has reached a big city. Another possibility is to migrate to another city, but the experience for those who have tried this generally indicates it is unlikely that conditions in another city will be better. The long-term alternative, one which administrators discuss, but which can only be realized far in the future—the simultaneous reduction of population and increasing of job opportunities—is a prospect too remote for those now living in cities even if it could be accomplished.

The prospects for the ordinary inhabitant of an urban area in a newly developing country is that things will be worse before they are better. A high degree of physical urbanization—in terms of *where* people live—is quite likely to be characterized by a low degree of social urbanization, in the sense of providing appropriate amenities for urban life.

The city in newly developing countries is always in flux. Now imperceptibly it is in flux: every morning a few more squatters' huts are found on the nearby hills. Now violently it is in flux, reluctantly serving as a receptacle for the sudden appearance of a million refugees in the partitioning of a country. Even in war it is in flux: the tide of events emptying it now and gorging it later, with conflict tearing at its structure and social fabric. Whatever the changes, it has a seemingly endless power to attract more and more people to the urban maw. What light can existing knowledge of urbanization throw on the changing city in newly developing countries? Just how applicable to such cities are established principles and theories about urban change? Most theories about the developing city arose from study of cities in the West; how useful are they for studying developments taking place in a quite different setting, and under conditions of rapid nationwide change? The question is further complicated by noting that under these circumstances the changing city may even be subject to deliberate intervention in the normal course of its development. Such factors inevitably affect the way in which cities grow, and presumably are related to the differences observable between Western and non-Western urbanization. In examining the non-Western urban area, it may be helpful to begin with a review of

CHAPTER FOUR

The Developing City

some of the standard models of urbanization and compare those with what is actually taking place in cities of newly developing countries.

GROWTH PATTERNS

Site and Situation

It is noticeable in urbanization everywhere that the factors of site and situation have considerable impact upon the nature of the urban area. *Site* refers to the actual physical characteristics of the location on which a city is built. *Situation* refers primarily to the relationship of a particular site to other parts of the area in which the city is located, to the region of which it is a part, and even, in many of the larger cities, to the nation and other nations.

The significance of site characteristics is suggested by Hong Kong, with its unique harbor facilities which provide a "natural" location for an urban area or a city to develop. What are favorable site characteristics from one point of view may, however, involve negative influences. In the case of Hong Kong the characteristics of site surrounding the harbor create certain difficulties with reference to urban development because of its rugged character. Or consider the site of Bombay, a peninsula protecting a vast harbor area, enabling it to deal with the foreign trade of India. But, as in the case of Hong Kong, the peninsular nature of Bombay has created some rather substantial difficulties in land transportation.

Lagos, capital of Nigeria, has a site that is most definitely inimical to development as a large urban area, being on an island. It has become necessary to compensate for this site characteristic by reclamation of land and special bridging to the mainland and other islands. This site characteristic, although it may not have adversely affected the early growth of Lagos, certainly has had an influence on both the direction of subsequent growth and the nature of growth in terms of population density and location, types of land use, and functional relationships from the point of view of transportation.

The situation of the city is also extremely important. It is clear, for example, in the case of Delhi that for hundreds of years a city has been in that location partly because the city stands at the head of the Gangetic Valley, and partly because this valley is the channel through which migrations and invasions into the Indian subcontinent traditionally have been made. It has been said that: "Whoever commands Delhi, commands India." Although the circumstances had changed by the time the British became intensively interested in India, it is quite probable that the symbolic importance of Delhi with reference to situation did not escape their notice, and may have influenced its eventual selection as the site of the new national capital in a suburb designated New Delhi.

Situational factors undoubtedly have influenced the growth of Bombay. Although the site characteristics are particularly important, Bombay's situation as the first accessible port to the commerce from Europe and Africa on the western side of the Indian subcontinent most certainly was instrumental in its development as a major port of India.

A host of illustrations of the importance of situation in urban areas of other newly developing countries can be adduced by reference to West Africa. Virtually all West African coastal cities are in their present positions because they served as crucial points of contact, not only for the collection and transshipment of goods from the interiors of the river systems at the mouths of which they are located, but also as points of access and distribution to the interior for products brought to these posts by sea from outside the country. Dakar, Abidjan, Accra, Lagos, and other West African urban areas serve as illustrations.

Calcutta, Bangkok, Singapore, Hong Kong—the list is endless—also reflect the importance of situation both with reference to the countries they serve on the mainland and their intercourse with trade from outside the country.

Kano, on the other hand, has served an extremely important role for both Nigerian areas and other parts of West Africa since it lies at a point between both the desert routes crossing the Sahara to the north and the coastal areas to the south. Kano has situational characteristics which are now being utilized in the air transportation age because of its unique location as an interchange point for both airline services in the West African area, and their linkage to routes connecting with Europe and the Mediterranean.

Growth Theories

Among the major theories of urban growth that have been advanced to account for the familiar characteristics of Western urban growth are those suggested by Richard M. Hurd, Ernest W. Burgess, Homer Hoyt, and Chauncy D. Harris and Edward L. Ullman. Although substantial modification may be required in applying them to the urban areas of newly developing countries, these theories serve as a useful point of departure, as indicated by the following summary of their major features.

Shortly after the turn of this century Richard M. Hurd published *The Principles of City Land Values* [1] in which he suggested—as a result of his

[1] Richard M. Hurd, *The Principles of City Land Values* (New York: Record and Guide, 1903).

observations of growth patterns in American and European urban areas—that cities tend to expand in concentric circles and in axial spokes along main transportation routes. At that time little attention was being paid to the whole question.

In 1923, Ernest W. Burgess [2] developed what has since become known as the zonal hypothesis of urban growth. Burgess theorized that, in the absence of any counteracting factors, the modern American city takes the form of five concentric, more or less symmetrical, rings or zones of development. Burgess referred to the most internal or central ring as zone 1, the central business district, the area of most intense community activity. Outside zone 1, Burgess noted what he called a transitional area, more or less concentric around the central business district. This area was assumed to be in the path of change and expansion from zone 1. Generally it was heavily populated, mostly by low-income and foreign groups, frequently with high personal and social disorganization, but it had relatively high land values in anticipation of the expansion of the central business district. Zone 3 Burgess called an area of working men's homes, occupied primarily by such persons as clerks and factory workers. Zone 4, the residential zone, tended to consist of dominantly single-family dwellings and local business districts, roughly 15 or 20 minutes by public transit from zone 1. Zone 5, the commuter zone, often located beyond the city limits and along the radial transportation lines, was located some 30 to 60 minutes by transit from the central business district and was the place of residence for high-income persons. It could also be the location of certain specialized districts such as manufacturing, railroad classification areas, and so on, mixed in with surviving agricultural areas.

The Burgess zonal hypothesis for explaining the patterns of American urban areas subsequently was subjected to heavy criticism. Maurice R. Davie pointed out, for example, that the central business district was not necessarily circular in shape, and commercial land use extended out radial streets and at subcenters as well as in the central business district. Continuing, Davie noted that industry was not located just in transitional areas, but also near rail and water facilities, wherever they were. Furthermore, he said that low-grade housing could be found in many parts of an urban area, especially near the industrial locations, with second- and first-class housing being almost anywhere else.[3]

[2] Ernest W. Burgess, "The Growth of a City," *Proceedings of the American Sociological Society,* **18** (1923), 85–89.

[3] Maurice R. Davie, "The Pattern of Urban Growth," in George P. Murdock, ed., *Studies in the Science of Society* (New Haven: Yale University Press, 1937), pp. 137–61.

Homer Hoyt developed the sector theory, another major theoretical approach to the explanation of growth patterns of urban areas.[4] In contrast to what Burgess had suggested, Hoyt observed that growth appeared to take place most rapidly along main transportation routes and along lines of least resistance.

The sector theory not only held that growth proceeds along particular axes of transportation but also that growth consists of extensions of the predominant type of land use in the particular corridor. Hoyt saw the city as a circle, various areas as sectors radiating out from the center, and similar types of land use as originating near the center and expanding outward toward the periphery.

In the mid-1940's geographers Chauncy D. Harris and Edward L. Ullman published what later came to be known as the multiple nuclei theory of urban growth, in which it was held that land-use patterns of urban areas develop around several discrete–*i.e.*, originally independent –nuclei, not around a single center.[5] These might be nuclei that have existed since the origin of the city or they may have arisen as a result of migration and specialization of different types of land use. Harris and Ullman pointed out four factors which in combination account for the rise of nuclei and the differentiation of districts of land use:

1. Certain activities require specialized facilities as, for example, retailing requires a high degree of accessibility, and manufacturing needs ample land and railroad service.
2. Like activities group together for mutual advantages, as in the case of the central business district.
3. Some unlike activities are mutually detrimental or incompatible with one another as, for example, the unlikelihood of high-income or high-status residential areas being located close to heavy industry.
4. Some uses such as storage and warehousing facilities, which have a relatively lower competitive capacity to purchase good locations, are able to "afford" only low-rental areas.

Obviously in any question as complex as growth patterns and development of urban areas, there have been numerous attempts to explain these phenomena. To date there is no one all-embracing theory that can be considered comprehensive or universally applicable.

[4] U. S. Federal Housing Administration, *The Structure and Growth of Residential Neighborhoods in American Cities* (Washington, D.C.: U.S. Government Printing Office, 1939); see also Homer Hoyt, "City Growth and Mortgage Risk," *Insured Mortgage Portfolio,* **1,** 6–10 (December 1936–April 1937).

[5] Chauncy D. Harris and Edward L. Ullman, "The Nature of Cities," *Annals of the American Academy of Political and Social Science,* **242** (November 1945), 7–17.

It is extremely difficult to determine the growth patterns of a newly developing country's urban areas, partly because there is seldom enough information available to determine whether the growth theories which have been useful in connection with Western urbanization are also applicable in other situations. It is reasonable to observe, however, that although these theories were created from observations of Anglo-European urbanization they are about as useful in non-Anglo-European cities. However, no one of the above theories is sufficiently applicable to serve by itself. Rather, with certain modifications, there exists what seems to be a concentric pattern of growth in the early stages of new cities, subsequently replaced—as was also true in the case of American urban areas—by a more nearly characteristic sector pattern of growth, although the multiple nuclei growth patterns in urban areas cannot be overlooked in either Western or non-Western cities. Some of the difficulties in studying non-Western urban areas in this connection result from insufficiency of data. Also some, in fact many, of these urban areas were extensively affected by the superimposition of foreign urban patterns on new cities. Urban growth by fiat, as in the case of New Delhi, India, is not likely to illustrate a "natural" urban growth process.

Certain background considerations must be kept in mind with reference to urban areas in newly developing countries. These cities experienced the greatest part of their growth up to very recent times in a situation where they were subject either to no controls or to controls less rigid than those in the United States today. In other words, most of these cities have grown virtually without zoning ordinances, subdivision regulations, building height controls or limits, and effective control over coverage of sites.

One notable exception to this general statement is the case of segments of new cities in newly developing countries reserved for settlement by foreign population. These segments frequently were laid out in a somewhat systematic pattern and were subjected to considerable building and land use regulations.

In addition to the haphazard conditions under which urban growth has taken place, there have been considerable unauthorized, that is, "squatter," settlement patterns and expansions within most of these cities or close to them. These have developed generally in a state of complete anarchy vis-à-vis the official establishment, although sometimes within certain self-imposed controls so as to preclude, for example, the blocking of pathways.

Certain observations can be made about what appear to be the major patterns of growth in these cities. For example, in cases where a very old city is the core, if there has been a history of defense wall-building the growth pattern tends to have been generally concentric until the protection walls became obsolete and were replaced either by further outlying walls, also generally concentric in pattern, or were not controlled by any new walls. Once the wall constriction on development is removed, the tendency is for radial growth to develop along major access routes.

In other cases where urban origins were the result of foreign influence—that is, the development of an urban area as a base of operation for either commercial or political exploitation of the country—cities tend to have planned cores surrounded by more or less haphazard growth of native settlements heavily influenced by radial access routes, with the native settlements early outstripping the foreign in both area and population.

Everywhere there is evidence of substantial influence of site characteristics on the growth pattern. Hong Kong, Bombay, Lagos, Istanbul, Khartoum, Abidjan, Freetown, and Cape Town are some of the cities that illustrate the important impact of both site and situation characteristics on urban growth patterns.

In each case it is also notable that where a foreign residential enclave exists it tends to pre-empt an entire area or segment outside an old city, and be planned with much more nearly open Anglo-European street pattern and amenities.

The patterns described above in very general terms do not necessarily apply to all urban areas in all newly developing countries. For example, the Latin American city stands in contrast to those of most other urban areas of newly developing countries. Partly because of the impact of regulations concerning the way in which cities should be developed under colonial supervision, and partly because of differences in culture and pattern in the Old World, the central part of a Latin American city very often was established and maintained as a high-prestige, high-value area. The typical pattern in association with this was the pushing of squatters and newcomers to the outskirts. The effect on land values and land ownership patterns of this major difference in Latin American cities, as compared with rapidly developing cities elsewhere, cannot be underestimated.

In Western urbanization individuals seeking urban residence have had a choice of cities in which to locate, and thus urbanization has been spread over a variety of sizes of places. In newly developing countries, the trek to the city may of necessity have been limited to one city, or only a few, thus focusing the burden of urbanization on a limited number of places and accentuating problems that otherwise could have been shared by many. Similarly, the rate of growth in most Western urban areas has been much more gradual—in terms of the number of years involved—as compared with the relatively rapid growth rates in many newly developing countries, with corresponding patterns that have emerged because of squatter settlement, large-scale refugee movements, and so on.

The growth patterns of many rapidly growing cities in newly developing countries have been influenced by their skipping certain "stages" that were common to much of Western urbanization. For example, most of these rapidly growing cities skipped the trolley-car stage, with all its implications for relatively compact development along major transport lines; the almost total absence of rapid mass transit facilities has also affected population distribution patterns.

With the exception of those parts of cities reserved for settlement by foreigners during colonial occupancy, the resulting urban growth and use patterns in newly developing countries tend to have been mostly haphazard, if not sometimes chaotic, and to reflect such circumstances as those mentioned above instead of studied attempts at urban planning.

ECOLOGICAL PROCESSES

The rapidly growing urban area does not just happen. It takes the form it presently has, has had in the past, and will have in the future, because of the operation of certain processes that permeate its growth.

Even though it may be impracticable to try to derive a single growth theory which can account for all phenomena in the urbanization of newly developing countries, the operation of ecological processes can be observed in the development of every urban area.

There is no general agreement as to the precise number of ecological processes that characterize or are exhibited in urbanization.[6] The traditional list of ecological processes consists of concentration, centralization, decentralization, segregation, invasion, and succession. In this discussion some of these traditional ecological processes will be combined or broken down into parts; furthermore, we will add the ecological process of routinization to the discussion. The ecological processes discussed seriatim are, in fact, operating in an urban area concurrently, perhaps at different rates of speed under different circumstances with one being

[6] R. D. McKenzie ("The Scope of Human Ecology," in E. W. Burgess, ed., *The Urban Community* (Chicago: University of Chicago Press, 1926), pp. 172–77), first fully stated the first six of these processes. For definitions of human ecology see: R. D. McKenzie, "Human Ecology," *Encyclopedia of the Social Sciences* (1931), V, 314; Amos Hawley, *Human Ecology: A Theory of Community Structure* (New York: The Ronald Press Company, 1950), p. 69; and James A. Quinn, *Human Ecology* (Englewood Cliffs, N.J.: Prentice-Hall, Inc., 1950), pp. 3, 68.

much more pronounced in its effect than another, only to be subsequently affected by the other ecological processes whose rates of development may in turn exceed that of the first one.

Whatever the ecological processes at work, there are certain background factors which affect their operation. Particular reference is made to the factors of competition and mobility.

The competitive factor is apparent in all of the ecological processes to be discussed and is, in effect, the origin of those processes. Competition for space derives from the fact that two objects cannot occupy the same space at the same time. It may be said that, to a large extent, the structure of an urban area—that is, the distribution of its population, its types of land use and functions—is a product of the competitive interaction of different population groups, land uses, functions, and institutions for positions in an urban area that will maximize the fulfillment of their requirements.

Mobility is measurable movement in a time or space framework, specifically, the movement of people and goods, land uses, and functional areas from one part of a city to another. It is so common to most of the ecological processes that virtually none can be understood unless mobility is considered as a component.

Variation in the nature and extent of mobility in urban areas has been closely related to the availability of various types of transportation facilities, for example, foot travel versus public mass transportation. Obviously the capacity for movement of goods and people is different in the case of travel by camel cart as compared with travel by truck or bus or a rail commuter system.

Concentration

The first of the seven ecological processes to be defined briefly is *concentration,* the process that results in the differential distribution of population in an urban area.[7] The focus is on residence, and the chief measure of the concentration process is in terms of population density. Factors affecting the process include differential access to transportation facilities and variations in economic capacity to purchase a place of residence or a location for a function or land use. A common result of the operation of the concentration process is the tendency of population density to be higher at or near the central parts of an urban area and progressively to decline as the periphery is approached. However, in newly developing countries, in addition to the heavy density central area there may be relatively high density squatter types of development at

[7] Quinn, *ibid.,* p. 333.

the periphery, not necessarily under the jurisdiction of the political unit in or adjoining which it occurs.

Centralization

The process of *centralization* relates to the focusing of functions around pivotal points of activity.[8] Dominance is the ordinary measure of the centralization process: the effect and relationship of the focusing of functions in particular areas on other parts of the urban complex. The development of the central business district serves as an illustration.

Decentralization

The process of *decentralization* refers to "the tendency for human beings and institutional agencies [as well as other types of land uses] to move away from the center of the city."[9] Mobility and competition are important factors in decentralization, which is most readily observed in the movement of population, commercial activities, and industry.

The relatively few large-scale industries in urban areas in newly developing countries are likely to be developed in a decentralized location rather than toward the center where congestion and inaccessibility of transportation facilities are not always conducive to easy operation. A great deal of the industry in these countries still tends to consist of relatively small units of operation, some of which originated and developed incidentally to other types of activities, and operate quite satisfactorily in the high density central parts of the urban area. This is typically performed in converted ground floors, back yards, upper stories of structures designed originally for residential use, and—when the weather permits—on nearby street areas. Adjoining buildings are invaded and makeshift shelters may also be used for expansion purposes.

Segregation

Segregation has traditionally been defined as the clustering or sorting out of land uses and population groups as resistance to the introduction of any disharmonious type of land use or population group.

Two types of segregation are differentiable: the first deals with the

[8] For variations in definition see Quinn, *ibid.*, p. 305; Stuart A. Queen and David G. Carpenter, *The American City* (New York: McGraw-Hill Book Company, 1953), p. 108; and Alvin Boskoff, *The Sociology of Urban Regions* (New York: Appleton-Century-Crofts, 1962), p. 118.

[9] A. B. Hollingshead, "Human Ecology," in Robert E. Park, ed., *An Outline of the Principles of Sociology* (New York: Barnes & Noble, Inc., 1939), p. 104.

segregation of like population units, that is, those having specific characteristics, and the second, termed "specialization," refers to nonpopulation-centered types of segregation.

The segregation involved in the sorting out of population groups is an extremely complicated process. Ordinarily segregation of population units has taken place with reference to such attributes as income, language, race, culture, or combinations of these factors. Population segregation is a partial result of conscious or unconscious preferences for associating with one group as compared with another, sometimes reflecting actual bias or prejudice. Such segregation may be accelerated or reinforced by the necessity of newly arriving, less-advantaged segments of the population to find a place of least resistance to their occupancy in an urban area; subsequently, in their efforts to secure housing elsewhere, such factors as income affect the capacity to afford a better location. The competition factor previously referred to is important in this connection. Further aspects of population segregation are discussed below in connection with the invasion process.

Specialization

A somewhat similar process exists in the nonpopulation-centered type of segregation, *specialization*, which involves the sorting out of uses, functions, and other types of activities in the urban area. Although related to population, they can be differentiated for purposes of discussion.

The principles of segregation and specialization involve the tendency of like units—either population or functional activities—to concentrate within a specific area.[10] Both segregation and specialization are predominantly along economic lines. The degree of homogeneity of segregation or specialization depends, among other things, on how long the processes have been at work, the significance of the attributes of selection—particularly their visibility—and, finally, the conditions of mobility affecting both population and nonpopulation units in the urban area. Segregation is not necessarily permanent; there is a constant shift or flux in the situation. In transitional areas at the borders of these differentiated population groups or land uses there is likely to be a very high mix or overlapping of population or use patterns.

The case study of Delhi, presented earlier for illustrative purposes, reveals that there is a much higher mix of land use and population groups in the cities of newly developing countries than in those of the West. This does not preclude the older parts of urban areas in newly

[10] See Hawley, *op. cit.*, Chaps. 13, 14.

developing countries from having had, from time to time, segregation of certain population segments in special quarters—areas which were restricted to occupancy by particular tribes, religious, income, or status groups of various sorts. In general there is a noticeably lower degree of population segregation in cities of newly developing countries than in Western urban areas, the major exception being in new high-grade residential suburbs that are virtually restricted to high-income segments of the population. In the days of colonial control of what are now newly developing countries, it was customary for the foreign population to be physically segregated from the local population. Another illustration of segregation, whether intentional or otherwise, is apparent in squatter residences developed on private or even public property and populated almost universally and exclusively by low-income, relatively unsophisticated, disadvantaged recent migrants to the urban area in newly developing countries.

Illustrations of specialization in urban areas of newly developing countries are beginning to emerge. The gradual establishment of planned industrial districts sorts out land uses that might otherwise have appeared indiscriminately throughout the urban area. The construction of new civic centers, particularly in national capitals, is leading to a sorting out of governmental functions into highly specialized areas.

Invasion

The *invasion* process is one of the most pervasive of all the ecological processes. Only those few cities which are not experiencing any kind of change seem to be free from its operation and effects. Invasion has been defined as "the penetration of a segregated area by an institutional function or population group different from the one already there," [11] and as "a sequence of spatial encroachment by an area of one type on the territory occupied by another type." [12]

The process of invasion has often implied the initiation of the displacement of a "higher" group or use by a "lower" one; however, a higher group sometimes drives out a lower one, thus also setting in motion a new cycle of invasion and succession. This virtually universal process in urban growth operates partly as a result of changes in the competitive relationships among different uses, institutional agencies, or population groups. The capacity of each for mobility is deeply involved. Invasion is the first stage in the succession cycle and it can affect all types of functions, land use, and population groups. Invasion of either population groups or different types of land use may be resisted or accelerated

[11] Hollingshead, *loc. cit.*
[12] Quinn, *op. cit.*, p. 358.

depending upon the attitude of the individuals involved, the owners, and government and private policy.

Conditions which initiate the invasion process include: population movement and expansion from one part of an area to another, or internally to an urban area; changes in the form and routes of transportation; obsolescence of housing resulting from physical deterioration or from changes in use; the erection of public or private structures having either attractive or repelling significance; the introduction of new types of industry or changes in the organization of existing types; changes in the economic base which may lead to a redistribution of income and affect the capacity of thc population to select and secure residences; and promotional activities such as government subsidy aid to encourage the public to locate its housing in a particular area, or to induce new or expanding industry to move to planned industrial districts.

The invasion of a different population group or another type of land use in an area is not an instantaneous process but passes through various stages. Pressure is the major force in the initial stage, such as the need for additional living space by an increasing population. The point of entry is frequently at the point of greatest mobility and resistance to it depends on the degree of solidarity of the occupants in the case of population, legal or quasi-legal restrictions ranging from zoning to private agreements, or the inertia of the type of land use which pre-exists the invading one.

Succession

If the invasion process continues, the original population group or use is gradually replaced. The climax of this invasion process is termed *succession,* sometimes differentiated as a separable ecological process, but in this discussion considered to be a part of the same invasion-succession cycle.

As has been noted, very seldom is there a 100 per cent completion of the invasion process.[13] However, complete invasion is often approached, and that stage may also be referred to as succession. If the invasion process is completed and there is a virtually 100 per cent replacement of one use or population group by another, this may be the end of the invasion-succession cycle, at least temporarily. This does not preclude that the newly invaded population group or use may not subsequently be replaced by another population group or use.

In urban areas of newly developing countries the most readily observable kind of invasion occurs when there is rapid extension of a built-

[13] *Cf.* Paul K. Hatt, "Spatial Patterns in a Polyethnic Area," *American Sociological Review,* **10** (June 1945), 352–56.

up area because of a population increase. The displacement of agricultural types of use by urban types of use, such as industry or residence—whether high-grade suburb or squatter development—is readily observable. Even some cases where newer parts of urban areas in newly developing countries have been planned illustrate the invasion process. For example, the eventual need for commercial facilities in connection with government housing or other projects may lead to taking over areas originally designed for residential purposes. Then, if the ultimate requirements exceed the capacity of a commercial area reserved for development, a gradual commercial invasion outside and in addition to the reserved area might be necessary.

Routinization

The process of *routinization* is defined as the daily movement of population back and forth from place of residence to place of daily activity, and of goods from point of origin to point of use.[14]

The highly systematized or routinized movement of people and goods in both Western and non-Western urban areas follows predictable patterns in terms of route taken and timing throughout the course of the day. There are also predictable weekly, seasonal, and even annual movement patterns.

Each working day witnesses the quite regular time to arise, the habitual route taken at the same time from place of residence to place of work or daily activity, the typical pattern of movement during the lunch hour, followed by the generally unvaried pattern of movement from place of work or activity back to the home.

Goods routinization refers to the regularized but different movements of milk, vegetables, meats, and fruit into an urban area and their stage-by-stage distribution from wholesaler to retailer to the individual who carries the groceries home at roughly the same time each day, or at least the same day of the week.

Venders appear on various streets at about the same time; street sweepers work at a highly predictable hour; factories and shops open and close at known times and receive deliveries of goods according to schedule; and the worshipper makes his way to shrine or mosque in a predictable pattern.

Routinization in Western urban areas differs from that in non-Western areas in type or degree partly as a result of variations in mix of land use, the predominant differences in place of work from place of residence, and variations in transportation facilities and other factors affecting movement. Nevertheless, there are discernible in every city—wherever

[14] See Hollingshead, *loc. cit.*, for an earlier and similar definition.

it is, no matter what its climate or characteristics—typical routinization patterns in movement of people and goods.

The operation of these ecological processes in cities of newly developing countries throws considerable light on the knowns and unknowns in the functional relationships among various parts of an urban area and the overall operation of the urban area. The operation of the ecological processes in cities of newly developing countries will vary, depending upon the part studied: the Old City, the recent growth areas, or the still-emerging areas likely to be at the periphery of the city's development.

The Old City, for example, is likely to exhibit a very slow rate of change in characteristics. It has a high intensiveness of use and function, a fine grain of different types of activities mixed together which, except for some specialized areas, is associated with a high mix of population. The typical short journey to work and closeness to all activities has interesting social implications, including the fact that Old City residents are more likely to live and be in direct participation with a larger mix of uses and population than is possible elsewhere in the urban area. The Old City also has differences of scale in terms of distance, size of shops, dwelling units, business operations, and industries. The Old City may be the "world of the man and the goods-carrying animal," instead of the world of the machine; associations and contacts are accordingly modified.

The Old City as described in Chapter Two and mentioned above does not necessarily exist in all newly developing countries. It is not as likely that—except for Yoruban in Nigeria—there will be the same kind of Old City in West African urban areas as in the Mediterranean, southeast Asia, Latin America, and the Indian subcontinent, where, in general, cities have existed for a longer time.

The operation of the ecological processes is influenced by differences in density patterns between Western and non-Western cities. Berry and his associates point out that as Western cities grow through time they tend to have a decreasing gradient of density and thus of compactness, with the central city densities first increasing and then decreasing.[15] Berry notes that this does not apply to non-Western urban areas. In Calcutta, for example, the central density increases but tends to remain high through time, there is nowhere near as great a decline in density toward the periphery, and the compactness of the city tends to remain high from a density point of view.

[15] Brian J. L. Berry, *et al.*, "Urban Population Densities," *Geographic Review*, **53** (July 1963), esp. pp. 400–401.

Nevertheless permanent recent peripheral high-grade growth areas—not new *squatter* settlements—in the cities of newly developing countries exhibit certain low density characteristics which affect the ecological processes. These include relatively fast rate of change, sparse population, and low intensity of land use, separation of uses and functions to a greater extent than elsewhere in the city, and isolation for all but the predominant use or population group from other parts of the city. In a sense these prestige areas represent a new world being built at the periphery of older urban areas, a world that is physically, culturally, and demographically different from the remainder of the city.

LAND USE, VALUES, AND OWNERSHIP

Land Use

Land use in urban areas of newly developing countries is an extremely interesting phenomenon and varies a great deal from that of Western urbanization.

In discussing land use in these cities of newly developing countries it is important to differentiate among various parts of the cities, especially the major sections that are likely to consist of (1) an "old city," (2) a "Western" area comprising suburbs, new central business district developments, and possibly new planned industrial districts, and (3) "squatter areas." Our objective is to call attention to the various factors that led to the existing land use pattern described in Chapter Two.

Several factors relate directly to the general characteristics of land use in urban areas of newly developing countries. Smaller lot size, particularly in the older parts of rapidly growing cities, multiplication of land uses, and larger size of family units in newly developing countries, tend to result in very high density. For example, a family with six members on a one-half-acre lot exists at a vastly different density from a family of six on a lot of only an eighth, a tenth, or a sixteenth of an acre. Multiplied many times over, such features account for some of the astonishingly high densities of population in the older parts of urban areas. Small lot size also results in higher density in commercial use measurable in terms of the number of shops per unit of area.

Certain kinds of land uses in cities of newly developing countries may have no fixed location or structure. A large number of activities take place directly on the street or in public places, whereas in a Western context they would occupy a specific piece of land. Sidewalk vendors spread out before them their small collection of goods, sometimes on consignment, available for purchase by the passerby. This is commercial land use, but such floating locations for business purposes are not devoted entirely to small retailers. For example, barbers frequently ply their trade in some quiet corner of a sidewalk or in any spot which can be pre-empted long enough to complete the shave or haircut. Similarly, in cities where bicycles are commonly used, a thriving repair business takes place in the open air.

Casual, that is, "unauthorized," markets for groceries and other kinds of goods frequently spring up in areas where there is a shortage of similar facilities in fixed locations. The non-Western equivalent of the taxi stand—for the rickshaw, tonga, or motorcycle "phut-phut"—has to be reckoned as a land use with a fixed location, irrespective of the fact that it is located on public property, the street. The "truck" terminal that makes its headquarters along the public curb, and piles upon the sidewalk the goods it has brought to the city, is another land use that in Western countries might be required to be off the street on its own property. These casual, though regular, business types of land use often must locate in the only place where they may be tolerated, rather than in what would be a prime location for their purpose.

To recapitulate, in general there is a much higher mix of land use in non-Western than in Western urban areas; the mix varies from place to place in the city, and the newer parts of the urban area are relatively more differentiated in land use than the older ones. For example, in the older parts of urban areas it is quite common to find residential, industrial, and commercial activities all taking place within the same block, perhaps even within the same cluster of houses or on the same lot. Often a storekeeper will live in his shop, a convenience that eliminates the journey to work and the need for additional clerks to continue his business during meal hours or when he is conferring with nearby shop owners.

Sometimes it appears that the only observable rational sorting out of land uses, particularly in the older parts of non-Western urban areas, is a vertical sorting in which ground floors of structures are used for commercial, office, or industrial purposes, but the second and succeeding stories are likely to be reserved for residential purposes. Obviously there are some modifications of this in certain areas, especially commercial, where the ground floor may be devoted to retailing, the next higher stories used for reserve stock storage purposes, and the upper stories devoted to residential use. This is quite in contrast with the horizontal separation of land uses to which the Westerner is accustomed.

The high mix of shops, small industries, and residential quarters in large parts of the non-Western urban area is also partly a result of the fact that in the case of commercial operations, for example, the predominant pattern is one of specialization. Supermarkets or large general stores supplying daily requirements are common in Western urban areas, whereas in non-Western cities virtually every shopkeeper has his specialty, making it necessary to have readily accessible a larger variety of shops. Specialization of function is undoubtedly related to the relatively small lot size that pertains in these urban areas.

Certain other types of uses, such as national centers for government offices, are becoming increasingly clustered, and areas are progressively being reserved for such purposes. This has met with varying degrees of success. Sometimes it appears that instead of following the objective of a unified area for governmental purposes, there may be occasions when a particularly propitious site for a prestigious or imposing structure will be chosen for that function rather than one closer to the other offices of government, irrespective of the dyseconomies involved.

The type of land use most likely to be differentiated from others is residential, particularly in the case of new areas for high-income groups which tend to be located at or near the periphery of the urban area. Here, Western patterns of separation of land use are more likely to be observed than elsewhere.

Unfortunately for large segments of the population in most non-Western urban areas the equivalent of a permanent residence is virtually nonexistent. Large proportions of the population are recent migrants and likely to be in the squatter category, living in hutments and various other temporary structures or, as in Rio de Janeiro, in a building under construction, in which workers are often permitted to live until it is completed.

One of the major land use problems for cities in newly developing countries is that of providing space for temporary residences for new migrants and for the swelling population of the city.[16] In Western urban areas the newcomer and the low-income individual are likely to settle in or close to the central business district or in other less attractive parts of the central city. In non-Western countries this pattern also pertains but, in addition, there is a heavy settlement of migrant population in temporary quarters both at the periphery of the urban area—sometimes referred to as the "septic fringe"—and in public and other temporarily vacant open spaces. Wherever these temporary residences are located, they are likely to lack services and to exhibit advanced degrees of squalor, filth, and degradation. They are not occupied by choice; the people are willing to live under extremely bad circumstances in hopes

[16] Lima Barreto's *Clara dos Anjos* is reported to be the "best account of unstable and marginal life of the suburbs of Rio de Janeiro in earlier parts of the century," according to Andrew Pearse, in UNESCO, *Latin America*. See also Oscar Lewis, *The Children of Sanchez: Autobiography of a Mexican Family* (New York: Random House, 1961), for life in a Mexico City slum.

of finding a foothold in the city that will lead to a better place to live. The universality of these squalid living quarters is suggested by the fact that virtually every country has a special name for them. The nearest Western equivalent is, perhaps, the "shanty towns" erected in various parts of the United States during the Depression years of the 1930's, although they were often far superior to those generally observable in newly developing countries, due to better construction, lower density, access to public facilities, and some public financial aid for building materials. In India squatter areas are called *bustees, jhuggies,* or *ahata,* in Tunis *gourbis* or *bidonvilles,* in Baghdad *sarifas,* in Brazil *favelas,* in Peru *borriadas,* in Venezuela *ranchos,* in Buenos Aires *villas miserarias,* in Sao Paulo *barrios,* in Porto Alegre *vilas de Malacas,* in Santiago *problaciones callampas,* in Colombia *barrios clandestinos,* in Caracas *cerros* or *quibradas*—one being built on steep hillsides and the other on ravines, in Mexico City *tugorios, jacales,* or *colonias proletarias,* referring respectively to one-room apartments opening on courtyards or passageways, shacks made of scrap metal, and plots of land secured from the government by pressure groups with better-constructed buildings but a shortage of facilities, and in Tripoli *barrakas,* filled with Bedouin squatters in traditional mud huts which are eventually made more substantial.[17]

Land Values

Almost everywhere different kinds of land uses are associated with varying land values which may be related to the types of operations taking place upon the property but also may reflect factors of land ownership.

There is a paucity of evidence on which to base generalizations about land values in the cities of newly developing countries. Even recent background studies, undertaken in connection with comprehensive plans for the largest and often only the capital cities, tend not to present information on land value trends over a long period of time. One reason is that land in these countries has been considered to be community property or, if privately owned, is so highly regarded as a possession that seldom is ownership transferred. This retards a study of land values which depends heavily on a record of transactions over a series of years, coupled with information about the kinds of use to which land was devoted, to indicate both the trends in land values and their present status.

Property transfer has been increasing in recent years, particularly

[17] The source of many of the above names is UN, *World Social Situation: 1957,* pp. 132, 180–87.

with the development of nationhood. Some property in urban areas that had been held for a long time by colonials for residential use was disposed of when they left the country or when there was a change in government. Where such lands were not acquired by the government, there is some record of property value.

The principles that control the value of land in Western urbanization seem to be at work in the case of non-Western areas. There is a relationship between land value and the type of use, the location of the particular parcel, and the associations related to it. One prominent feature involves the important role of custom and tradition in the new countries, a tradition which is often related to a longer history than the history of the country as a nation. "Sentiment and symbolism" are as relevant to land values here as in the West.[18] For example, the "old family" which "has always lived there" may be extremely reluctant to dispose of its property except for a high price, and sometimes not even then. Positional status considerations such as proximity to the home of the ruling government official may have an influence on the value of a piece of property; in some cases, this location may be precisely the same as earlier when the native ruler, prior to nationhood, lived in the same quarters. As in Western urbanization, proximity to particular places or to certain institutions may have a strengthening or weakening effect on the value of the land, depending upon the point of view of the individual owning it and the importance of the institution or use. Proximity to a mosque, for example, might have a very high rating factor in terms of land value for a Moslem, but a negative factor for one of another faith not requiring access to such a facility.

It is interesting to note the emergence of Western criteria for differentials in land values. Where modern central business districts have been developed, or are replacing the older style, great importance is attached to their accessibility to the population, as in the case of Western cities. Similarly, high income members of the population seeking high prestige sites for new homes may find that land values near diplomatic enclaves or residences of their own government officials reflect the scarceness of such desirable areas.

The patterning of land values in these rapidly growing countries is affected by the failure of these countries to support an established land value by land-use control devices such as zoning. Lightning may strike by fiat and bring wealth or loss depending upon, for example, a governmental decision to construct a new public building on a particular site, to establish new transportation facilities that pass or bypass the location,

[18] Walter Firey, "Sentiment and Symbolism as Ecological Variables," *American Sociological Review,* **10** (April 1945), 140–48.

or, in the case of outlying areas, to extend water and sewer lines to or beyond the area under discussion.

Land Ownership

Land ownership is of considerable importance in land values. In non-Western urban areas the question of land ownership frequently becomes quite complex because of shared or hereditary ownership of particular pieces of property. For example, in Lagos, one of the problems encountered in securing sites for rebuilding and adding to the central business district was the acquiring of land owned by a tribe, whereupon it became very difficult to ascertain whether the land could be sold! In many cases titles are not clear, partly because there has been no practice of registration of title—a fairly sophisticated and recent development even in Western countries. Even if "everyone knows" who owns a piece of land, modern transactions require more precise statement of ownership than is represented by this kind of designation.

Absentee ownership of land becomes important in non-Western countries for the same reasons as in Western countries, for example, when parcels of property must be assembled into one large piece to permit redevelopment, clearance, or other large-scale ownership. It also permits a considerable degree of tolerance of squatter development on relatively valuable land not in permanent use. Moreover, absentee ownership has implications for the types of relationships among people in urban areas. For example, if an absentee owner rents his property he may have a considerable impact on the kinds of people who can occupy particular places, as well as the obligations which the tenant may have toward the absentee owner rather than toward the municipality of which he is a part.

In non-Western countries the government is apt to control, or own, large parts of an urban area. This may effectively freeze vacant land for permanent types of use until the government is ready to exploit it, making it accessible in the meantime for occupancy by squatters. On the other hand, extensive government ownership of land is advantageous because generally there are no zoning or subdivision regulations or other controls which would have a salutary influence on the development of the property if it were privately owned. There is a definite net advantage to government ownership when it leads to reservation of property, temporarily preventing any development. Furthermore, when such land comes into use it can be assumed to be used in the best possible way. In some cities, as in Delhi, a large part of the peripheral land is owned by the government, thus providing a potential for controlling the rate and direction in which development may take place. In some countries, such as Egypt, until fairly recent times it has been the custom for quasi-public or private organizations to assume the ownership of property donated to it for philanthropic purposes. Such was the case of the religious *waqf* which, in pre-revolutionary Egypt, controlled a substantial portion of the land in the older part of Cairo, as well as land at the periphery. These properties are now undergoing a transfer to other holders, including the government.

It is interesting to speculate what future patterns of land values and land ownership will develop as a result of changes in land use associated with the rapid growth of these urban areas. The directions are not yet entirely clear, and the varying roles of tradition internal to the country, experience that may be borrowed from the West, and innovations still to be created are yet unknown.

THE MECHANICS OF URBAN LIFE

Urban areas can neither exist nor survive with mere reference to the ideals and objectives which are created to go along with them. Instead there must be a minimum, and preferably an optimum if not a maximum, of certain mechanics, supplies, and services in urban areas to make these areas most productive and gratifying. We refer in particular to facilities and services such as water, sewers, transportation, markets, food handling, and housing. These subjects are discussed with reference to the following: requirements involved, capabilities or resources available, some major problems associated with the provision of facilities and services, and finally, the main question of housing and related facilities.

Requirements and Capabilities

The plight of urban areas faced with the demands placed upon them is not an enviable one. The real dimensions of the requirements that they face are not entirely clear, partly because of the unpredictably rapid rate of growth. In fact, in most cases urban requirements are not yet even calculated; if they were, they would inevitably appear to be outpaced by in-migration to urban areas, a flow which appears to continue unabated irrespective of the urban area's capacity to deal with it.

As a result there are major shortcomings in the capacity of urban areas to cope with the pressing demands. Sometimes this is magnified by unfortunate early errors in the provision of basic facilities. For example, in one city a major installation for a drinking water system was located too close to a major sewage outlet, with the result that when the water level was low and the stream pressure was therefore reduced, sewage backed up into the intake pipe for the water supply, thus leading to a major outbreak of hepatitis. This poor planning, not to mention the difficulties that resulted from the illnesses connected with it, was compounded by the fact that the early planning interfered with constructing a proper major water system which later had to be developed to take care of the increasing population of the urban area.

Perhaps the basic difficulty in providing facilities and services for metropolitan areas in newly developing countries is that settlement areas ordinarily are vastly greater than those covered by inadequate public potable water supply, sewage collection, and waste transportation systems, as well as public transportation facilities. These complex, high-capital-cost facilities are very difficult to provide rapidly enough to catch up with the demand.

Unfortunately the resources and capabilities available to such metropolitan areas for coping with these difficulties are likely to be extremely limited. The major problem is that the supply of technical know-how is ordinarily not adequate for the task in hand, not because individuals themselves may not be competent, but because the job is too large for the small number of technically trained personnel. West Africa, on the other hand, has neither a large supply of college-trained individuals nor enough technical universities to train adequate numbers of engineers, even though West African countries might wish to produce them. As a result these countries have had to resort to training outside the country, which correspondingly leads to some loss of personnel from the country, both in terms of absence and occasional failure to return to work in the country upon completion of training.

In addition, the typical newly developing country finds itself in short supply of appropriate materials, rolling stock for its transportation system, pipes for sewage and water supply systems, cement for reinforcement of construction, and steel.

In some respects the major difficulty is that of financial resources. Virtually all investments in utilities and services are heavy ones and have to be financed in such a way as to permit the costs to be spread out over many years. Capital must be available in large blocks in order to ensure an adequate and carefully designed system, including expansion capacity contingency. The financial resources of most urban areas in newly developing countries appear to be hopelessly inadequate. In fact, most countries find their problem still further complicated by the generally low capacity of the ordinary citizen to be taxed for funds to meet the needs of public services and utilities. The great majority of citizens who come to urban areas are not even able to purchase housing, let alone be taxed heavily enough to produce sufficient revenue for installation of conveniences and services.

Public Transportation

The facilities and services required for urban living include drinking water, sewers, transportation, markets, and housing. It is not possible in this short discussion to cover each of these subjects. However, for illustrative purposes, special attention will be paid to mass public transportation and to housing.

Providing mass transportation facilities for cities in newly developing countries is an extremely costly and complex problem. It is complicated partly by the legacy of generally unimproved circulation systems that characterize many parts of these metropolitan areas. It is only in rare cases that pre-existing street systems are adequate for, or adaptable to, modern circulation requirements of rapidly growing cities. There may be a few properly prepared and organized traffic arteries, but vast areas of these cities remain relatively unserved even in terms of adequate paving, let alone the provision of vehicles for mass public transportation. The problem is further complicated because automobile and truck traffic is a relatively small proportion of the total, whereas it predominates in Western urbanization. Traffic here is a nightmare mixture of many modes of transportation: camelcarts, trucks, bicycles, horses, donkeys, buses, railroads, pedestrians, motorcycles, rickshaws, tongas, and various others. This mix of modes of transportation involves travel at greatly varied speeds and virtual disregard for channelization. The pedestrian carrying a heavy load on his back has to compete with the lurching overloaded bus that tries to get through the traffic by blowing its horn louder than the horn of the truck just behind it. The number of pedestrians using rights-of-way is much greater than anything conceivable to the ordinary resident of Western urban areas. Walking is still part of the way of life in newly developing countries.

The movement of people, as compared with the movement of goods, is complicated partly because of the wide variety of vehicles available for this purpose, and partly because of the poor equipment ordinarily provided for mass transportation systems. It is not unusual for perhaps up to 35 or 40 per cent of the rolling stock of a public bus system to be incapacitated at one time and to be in the repair shops, awaiting either spare parts or mechanics competent to make repairs and put the vehicles back on the street. Private vehicular transportation virtually does not exist for the vast majority of the urban population which usually walks, rides in the public transportation system as often as the fare is available, or occasionally is able to hire a tonga or rickshaw.

In some urban areas the topography may permit widespread use of the bicycle. This considerably ameliorates the transportation problem because of the relatively low investment required. Nevertheless, the cost of a bicycle is significant, considering the low average annual wages of the vast majority of the residents in non-Western urban areas.

The moving of goods is undertaken by every device known to man, including man himself. Transportation of light goods by human pack carrier is progressively declining, being gradually replaced by the use of wagons, light trucks, or animal transportation. The goods that float down the Nile on a *felûka* or come into the harbor of Hong Kong on a junk are most likely to be transported to a warehouse by human strength rather than by machine, and are ordinarily distributed still further by human carriers. Long-distance hauling and major bulk distribution internally to the urban area increasingly tends to be provided by the ubiquitous Mercedes truck or some similar vehicle able to survive the strains placed upon it by overloading, 24-hour use, and irregular maintenance. First-rate rail commutation and express service are rare and beyond the purse of most residents, though occasionally, as in Bombay, lower-class coaches are available.

Comprehensive plans for circulation systems and specifications for vehicles to establish and maintain the system exist in substantial numbers. The major difficulty is that of finance, the resources being inadequate to provide the kinds of circulation facilities required. Nevertheless, goods do move and people do get from place to place, albeit with considerable inefficiency and—for low-income urban residents—at considerable cost.

Housing

One of the thorniest problems of rapidly growing urban areas is shelter. Like employment shortages, housing has significant economic, social, and political ramifications. The highly visible implications of inadequate housing are apparent even to the most hardened visitor to newly developing countries; officials responsible for resolving the housing problem place it among the highest in priority.

Charles Abrams [19] and other students of housing in newly developing countries conclude that there exists under these circumstances a housing deficit of astonishing proportions, doubtless underestimated, and progressively greater as a result of the increased in-migration of population and the overuse of the existing housing supply—which accelerates its deterioration and removal from use.

[19] Charles Abrams, *Man's Struggle for Shelter in an Urbanizing World* (Cambridge, Mass.: Massachusetts Institute of Technology Press, 1964). Abrams' book is an exceptionally well written, comprehensive, and authoritative analysis, based on extensive firsthand experience and study.

The deficit is almost unbelievable. It results partly from the chronic overcrowding which has taken place in such urban areas over a long period, and partly from the traditional obligation to take in relatives who are new arrivals. This deficit is further accentuated by the frequently low level of repair that characterizes much urban housing, and by some housing destruction incidental to redevelopment in connection with the building of modern central business districts and government projects.

The final factor of great importance in this problem is the extremely low capacity of the economy to compensate by the construction of government—*i.e.*, public—housing. The rate of growth of the problem is so great that it seems inconceivable that any of the countries discussed here can hope to catch up with the demand. Even in the case of Hong Kong, where a truly massive attack has been mounted to cope with the housing problem, the thousands of government units already constructed are still only a minute proportion of the large number of dwelling units required.

Besides the seemingly insuperable financial problem, there are other dimensions which must not be overlooked. One is the vexing question of how to *produce* structures even if more nearly adequate funds were available. The chronic shortage of many critical building materials and the dependence of builders on hand labor inevitably affect the rate of production of housing units. There is a serious deficit, also, in community facilities and services required, or desirable, in connection with the additional housing being provided.

In some newly developing countries, one underlying difficulty in solving the housing problem centers around a shortage of both professionally trained and experienced staff in this field and supporting services or administrative devices to frame and carry out a viable program. Furthermore, as in almost every country of the world, it is generally impossible to interest private enterprise in supplying housing for low-income people. The major responsibility for such housing thus becomes that of the government, which is already burdened with other crucial problems of development. Housing must compete with other government jobs for priority in funds, staff, and execution. The dimensions of the housing task are suggested in Table 10, which provides estimates of annual need for the period 1960–1975.

The compilers of Table 10 include the following among their comments on this table:

> The table summarizes the annual housing requirements in the developing continents in the 15 years to 1975. By 1965, a total annual output of nearly 24 million dwellings would be required, on the assumption of replacing exist-

Table 10

Annual Housing Needs of Africa, Asia and Latin America: 1960–75 *

(In millions of dwelling units)

Categories of housing need	1960		1965		1970		1975	
	Urban	Rural	Urban	Rural	Urban	Rural	Urban	Rural
I. Population increase								
Africa	0.3	0.54	0.4	0.67	0.5	0.73	0.7	0.8
Asia	1.9	3.40	2.6	3.70	3.5	4.30	4.8	4.6
Latin America	0.8	0.30	1.0	0.20	1.2	0.20	1.5	0.2
II. Elimination of deficit or shortage over 30 years								
Africa	0.13	0.60	0.13	0.60	0.13	0.60	0.13	0.60
Asia	0.80	4.00	0.80	4.00	0.8	4.0	0.8	4.0
Latin America	0.30	0.30	0.30	0.30	0.3	0.3	0.3	0.3
III. Replacement of stock over								
A. 30 years (urban) and 20 years (rural)								
Africa	0.13	0.9	0.13	0.9	0.13	0.9	0.13	0.9
Asia	1.10	6.0	1.10	6.0	1.1	6.0	1.1	6.0
Latin America	0.40	0.5	0.40	0.5	0.4	0.5	0.4	0.5
B. 50 years								
Africa	0.078	0.36	0.078	0.36	0.078	0.36	0.078	0.36
Asia	0.68	2.44	0.68	2.44	0.68	2.44	0.68	2.44
Latin America	0.236	0.21	0.236	0.21	0.236	0.21	0.236	0.21
C. 100 years								
Africa	0.039	0.180	0.039	0.18	0.039	0.18	0.039	0.18
Asia	0.340	1.220	0.34	1.22	0.34	1.22	0.34	1.22
Latin America	0.118	0.115	0.118	0.115	0.118	0.115	0.118	0.115
I. Population	3.00	4.24	4.00	4.570	5.20	5.23	7.00	5.60
II. Deficit	1.23	4.90	1.23	4.900	1.23	4.90	1.23	4.90
III. Replacement								
A. 30-20 years	1.630	7.400	1.63	7.40	1.63	7.40	1.63	7.40
B. 50 years	0.994	3.010	0.994	3.01	0.994	3.01	0.994	3.01
C. 100 years	0.497	1.505	0.497	1.505	0.497	1.505	0.497	1.505
Total								
A.	5.860	16.540	6.860	16.870	8.060	17.530	9.860	17.900
B.	5.224	12.150	6.224	12.480	7.424	13.140	9.224	13.510
C.	4.727	10.645	5.727	10.975	6.927	11.635	8.709	12.005

Rate per 1000 inhabitants in 1965	Urban	Rural	Total
A.	13.6	9.5	10.4
B.	12.3	7.0	8.2
C.	11.3	6.2	7.3

* *Source:* United Nations Department of Economic and Social Affairs, *Report of Ad Hoc Group of Experts on Housing and Urban Development* (New York: United Nations, 1962), p. 61. For full discussion of the table see Annex III, pp. 60, 62.

ing stock in 30 years in urban areas and 20 years in rural areas. With replacement periods of 50 years and 100 years, the annual requirements in new dwellings by 1965 would be 20 million and 17 million respectively or, allowing for "reconditioning" needs with the longer replacement periods, 21.7 million and 19.3 million respectively. An overall annual housing programme of 8 to 10.4 dwellings per 1,000 inhabitants is, therefore, required in these continents, depending on the rate at which existing dwellings are replaced.

This may be compared with the housing outputs currently being attained in the other more advanced regions of the world, *e.g.*, Europe and North America. An annual rate of 8 or more dwellings per 1,000 inhabitants is currently [1960] being attained only in Sweden (9.1), Switzerland (9.3), the Federal Republic of Germany (10.5), and the U.S.S.R. (14.0). In the United States, France, Finland, the Netherlands, and Norway, the current rate is from 7.0 to 7.5 dwellings per 1,000 inhabitants. The other countries of Europe currently provide from 4.0 to 6.5 dwellings annually per 1,000 inhabitants.[20]

URBAN PLANNING IN NEWLY DEVELOPING COUNTRIES

For persons familiar with the scale and nature of planning problems in newly developing countries it is axiomatic that the greater the growth problems, and the more limited the resources to cope with them, the more logical—and essential—it is to plan for maximizing whatever effective action is possible. Problems of urban development can be effectively dealt with best by planning.

The climate that pertains for national planning in most newly developing countries not only tends to be good, but ranges to perfect. However, for urban planning there may be considerable doubt as to whether attitudes are favorable to its existence and, particularly, to its practice. In spite of what presumably would seem to be an obvious logical extension of the national planning process, urban planning appears to stand considerably down the list of priorities. In some cases it is either entirely absent or just getting under way; in any case urban planning is very late and not broad enough.

Status of Plans for Urban Areas

Examination of the present status of plans for urbanization in many newly developing countries reveals a great gulf between the objectives for such planning and the practice. Although some countries have a pol-

[20] United Nations, Department of Economic and Social Affairs, *Report of Ad Hoc Group of Experts on Housing and Urban Development* (New York: United Nations, 1962), p. 62. See also *Report of the 1963 Working Party on Government Policies and Practices with Regard to Squatters, Resettlement, and Government Low Cost Housing* (Hong Kong: Government Printing Office, 1963).

icy that all cities over a certain size—and this varies with the country—are expected to complete plans before a specified date, it is clearly impossible for cities to meet this requirement. This follows partly from the unavailability of trained professional planning staff, partly because of the unacceptability, or lack of capacity or interest, in meeting the planning requirements, and partly from the ubiquitous additional factor of the shortage of funds to do anything about the plans. These encourage a "Why plan?" attitude.

In those cities for which plans have been completed the situation may be expected to be better but, in fact, it may not be substantially different.

In many cases—*e.g.*, Bangkok, Delhi, and Tema—the preparation of comprehensive master plans for urban areas has been undertaken with special interest. Some plans have been prepared by staffs of nationals usually heavily assisted by foreigners imported for the purpose. There is an almost inevitable and predictable suspicion of any such plan. The difficulty is that any plan in which a foreigner participates is bound to be questioned as to its pertinence and viability. It automatically suffers the potential curse of any conflicts of culture standards and objectives that may have derived by virtue of having an "outsider" participate in its preparation. Unfortunately it appears that some of the plans prepared, whether with foreign staff aid or otherwise, are unrealistic in terms of feasibility. The proposals may be extremely logical but impracticable in view of the limited financial, leadership, and technical capacities of the countries and cities involved.

The fate of many plans is not surprising. For example, a plan may go "on the shelf" with little impact upon the actual situation. The completed plan, no matter how good it may be, often gets so thoroughly emasculated in the draft review by the myriad officials who feel compelled to comment upon it that it ends up with practically all of its significance, balance, and comprehensiveness removed.

Nevertheless, even if the first and second problems have been encountered, it is generally felt that at least there may be certain fringe, if not direct, benefits involved in the planning process. Perhaps, for example, the public works department or other officials will be converted to the concept of comprehensive planning—that is, considering related factors in anticipating the kinds of problems which may be faced in the near and distant future—rather than working on a provincial and *ad hoc* day-to-day basis.

Professional Planning Staff

One of the greatest difficulties confronting newly developing countries is the serious shortage of nationals professionally trained to undertake the urban planning. The result is that these countries frequently send their promising individuals abroad for professional planning training, and expect them to return to their country of origin equipped to deal with national problems at the urban level. Inevitably the upshot of such training abroad—using Western examples—is the importation of foreign planning notions, which are likely to be inapplicable to the context in which the returning national may find himself.

Another alternative, which to date has been experimented with only on a very limited scale, is to provide indigenous professional planning schools with visiting foreign professors selected for their ability to adapt themselves and their planning knowledge and skills to the problems of particular developing countries. Unfortunately, only the very large countries such as India have found it possible to support a professional planning program for experts on urban affairs.

Theory and Practice: Additional Considerations

Modifications in theory and techniques are obviously required in urban planning for newly developing countries. Many of the research techniques considered highly useful in Western environments are still quite patently inapplicable in newly developing countries. The discerning consultant rapidly learns this, and discovers that he must develop new research techniques that can be made operable in foreign situations characterized by limited data and relatively untrained staff to manipulate these data. New formulas or new solution procedures have to be contrived and applied readily and successfully to the new situation. Furthermore, a new consciousness of urban planning among officials, hitherto satisfied to work only within their own bailiwicks, must be encouraged, including an attitude toward coordination and collaboration of fellow experts in the local context. One extreme example of the necessity for developing techniques applicable to the local situation is the relatively futile effort to construct viable models for the development of urbanization in newly developing countries, a device which is extremely popular in the West. Few, if any, of the Western models fit most newly developing countries; none has really worked well yet. A quite different model must be formed if it is to be applicable to the urban situation in newly developing countries.[21]

[21] Matters of transferability of technical skills, practices, and standards from highly developed to less-developed countries have been explored in some detail in Gerald Breese, "Research and Data Requirements for Urban Comprehensive Master Planning in Rapidly Developing Countries," in *Urbanization in Old and New Countries*, proceedings of a series of lectures (Durban, South Africa: Institute for Social Research, University of Natal, 1964), Vol. I, pp. 43–58.

Questions of Policy

A full explanation of the process of urban planning cannot be given here. There remain, however, certain generally relevant questions of policy which may be raised to assist in understanding the nature of urban planning in newly developing countries. Do the few planning experts themselves know well enough what ought, can, and will be done in urban area planning? Is there, by definition, such a gulf between professionals and the urban public in newly developing countries that there can be no effective communication? The answer to this question is very crucial because in such countries there is little public participation in the planning process to act as a check on professional judgment and decisions. There is desperate need for establishing "watchdog" citizen groups to fill this vacuum in the planning process.

The question of whether control of urban development is best accomplished by government ownership of only developable land, government ownership of all land, or no government ownership is a serious policy issue.[22] In any case, policy must be established as to what type and intensity of control will be placed on forthcoming urban development and existing developed land in terms of availability for use; type, intensity, and differentiation of use; and type of ownership to be permitted.

Another question of policy reflects an interest in the ability of newly developing countries to avoid some of the mistakes that have been made in Western countries. When and under what circumstances will it be possible for central cities and various parts of their conurbations to receive practical, effective powers from national governments to act together in planning? It is conceivable that if large enough administrative units are placed at the disposal of urban planners, many of the errors and shortcomings of contemporary planning for metropolitan area development in the West can be avoided.

Another policy question pertains to the extent to which urban development should receive a newly developing country's attention and resources in view of other large and competing demands of national and rural development. What are to be the investment policies of the nation regarding promotion of industrialization in general versus overall urbanization, the demands of the capital city as compared with other cities. and the relationship of a few major cities to all cities in the newly de-

[22] The entire subject of New Towns—not discussed here—illustrates one question of policy to be decided. See Frederic J. Osborn and Arnold Whittick, *The New Towns: The Answer to Megalopolis* (London: Leonard Hill, 1963), esp. Chap. xi, "Achievement, Emulation, and Prognostic." Pp. 141–48 list New Towns in various parts of the world, including about 50 in Africa, 106 in Asia, 8 in Australia, 71 in Europe, 51 in North America, and 8 in South America.

veloping country? When countries with even vast resources cannot find sufficient funds and skills to allocate to all problems they face it becomes quite apparent that these questions of investment policy are even more crucial for newly developing countries, most of which are endeavoring, among other things, to establish themselves on a firm financial footing.

Among the policy questions noted above is to what extent it is a wise, long-term practice to siphon the bulk of national growth supports to the biggest cities in a developing country, in contrast to a general, overall decentralization effort involved in building up small cities and industrialization over a wider area. This ranks as one of the two or three major issues in national policy; it is clear that this is not a simple policy to determine. Much industrialization, and in particular, heavy industrialization, depends on the creation or development of a large complex of interrelated services, facilities, professional personnel, equipment, and other relevant factors essential to efficient operation. It may very well be that a small, newly developing country cannot afford to provide such resources in more than one or two locations at any one time. This infrastructure is much more crucial than may be evident on first examination. It is perhaps this factor, as much as any other, which has influenced investment in industrialization to focus on a relatively small number of cities rather than to disperse more widely. There appears to be no escape from the necessity to have a strong infrastructure of services and supporting industries if reasonably large-scale industrialization is to be undertaken. This is the problem of "critical mass" of industrialization and urbanization in small cities. Judging from experience to date, these issues have not yet been completely and successfully resolved. Just how wisely they are resolved, temporarily and finally, is obviously of great significance to urbanization in newly developing countries.[23]

[23] See United Nations, *Report of the Ad Hoc Group of Experts on Housing and Urban Development,* and Abrams, *op. cit.,* for generally good background material related to these and other policy questions.

Having discussed the scale and pace of urbanization, the role of the city in newly developing countries, the kinds and characteristics of emerging urbanization with particular reference to the variety and morphology of cities in newly developing countries, the characteristics of the inhabitants of urban areas, and the nature of the developing city in newly growing countries, it is now appropriate to review the evidence and attempt some observations, and perhaps conclusions, regarding the shape of things to come in the urbanization of countries undergoing modernization throughout the world.

We will first discuss the general question of overurbanization and then examine various projections that have been made with reference to the growth of rapidly urbanizing areas, raising the question as to whether the past is a prologue to the future, posing further questions, and making certain observations about what appear to be the most likely prospects, subsequently calling attention to some of the policy implications involved. We will conclude with some general comments about the relationship of the city to the nation in newly developing areas.

OVERURBANIZATION

From time to time in the course of this review of urbanization, attention has been called to the question of *overurbanization.*

CHAPTER FIVE

The Shape of Things to Come

Claims and counterclaims regarding the existence of overurbanization appear frequently in the literature for it constitutes one of the many major issues that interest both students observing these phenomena and policy makers in countries undergoing rapid urbanization. This is a perennial question, and although we may not find a definitive answer, perhaps some light will be shed on the various dimensions and ramifications involved.

Overurbanization is generally defined in terms involving a situation in which "larger proportions of . . . [a country's] population live in urban places than their degree of economic development justifies."[1] This phenomenon has been noted with particular interest and concern because of the common observation, in newly developing countries, that with very few exceptions there appears to be much too large a population in urban areas to be supported by the employment, services, and facilities available. The concern displayed reflects the observation of Western countries, as compared with newly developing countries, that at similar stages of urbanization in Western countries there was a much higher degree of participation of the labor force in occupations that were urban in character, *i.e.*, nonagricultural.

Urbanization in newly developing countries is taking place at an unusually rapid pace. However, it may be that what is considered overurbanization from one point of view may not be from another. For example, to the outside observer, overurbanization may appear to exist if measured in terms of job availability; on the other hand, a situation may not be classed as overurbanization from the point of view of a country seeking rapid growth on a national scale—although here, too, rapid growth may appear to be beyond a country's capacity for achieving that growth.

It is extremely difficult to define or delineate the point at which overurbanization exists or is claimed to exist. Is it when the proportion of the total population in cities is higher than might otherwise be expected? Is it when there is too great an urbanization in a few cities, as compared with the same quantity of urbanization spread over many cities? Do we use the term overurbanization for only some segments of the urban population, and not others? Can there be overurbanization for only the unskilled members of the labor force? Does overurbanization apply to land and sites on which people can build homes, and the

[1] Philip M. Hauser, "The Social, Economic, and Technological Problems of Rapid Urbanization," in Bert F. Hoselitz and Wilbert E. Moore, eds., *Industrialization and Society* (Paris: UNESCO and Mouton, 1963), p. 203. *Cf.* N. V. Sovani, "The Analysis of 'Overurbanization,'" *Economic Development and Cultural Change,* **12** (January 1964), 113–22.

capacity of the economy to provide such homes? Can we measure overurbanization in terms of supporting population at a standard of living that is attractive to the Western world, or should the degree of overurbanization be measured in terms of standards of the developing country? The utility of each of these criteria and others for measuring the existence, extent, and significance of overurbanization varies from place to place and carries different weights depending upon the expert making the assessment.

One concomitant of overurbanization appears to be a similar kind of overruralization. As the United Nations *Report on the World Social Situation: 1957* indicated:

> The pressure of population on land, which contributes to what is judged to be overurbanization in so many of the less-developed countries, means, however, that these same countries are in a similar sense "over-ruralized"; *i.e.*, there are too many people for the existing modes and levels of production in both the urban and rural sectors. Both sectors are economically underdeveloped; "overurbanization" is but another way of describing the economic underdevelopment that characterizes the cities and their relation to the countryside.[2]

The extent to which this situation may exist is suggested by Harley L. Browning, who reports a –0.96 correlation between the overurbanization of certain countries and the overruralization of the same countries. Browning contends that "the real solution to this problem does not lie in reducing the urban population, but in increasing it,"[3] *i.e.*, manpower may be used ineffectively in both urban and rural situations. While the prescription may in theory be good, so far it has not worked too well. The general conclusion seems to be that there is a close relationship between overurbanization and economic underdevelopment, and only a solution to the latter problem will resolve the question of overurbanization.

One of the concerns here is the risk that urban areas—especially the capital, primate, or most politically troublesome ones—may have diverted to them too great a share of a nation's finance, manpower, and talent resources that might be used more productively elsewhere in the economy. This point has been discussed elsewhere in the present study. The question that arises is: Under what conditions is urbanization an ac-

[2] UN, *World Social Situation: 1957*, p. 124.

[3] Harley L. Browning, "Recent Trends in Latin American Urbanization," *Annals of the American Academy of Political and Social Science*, **316** (March 1958), p. 117, esp. note 6.

celerator of economic development, and under what conditions can it be considered a decelerator of economic development? The answers are by no means clear, and will doubtless vary from country to country.

Fortunately, it is unlikely that overurbanization in underdeveloped countries can last too long. The end of overurbanization may take place because of a breakdown in the capacity of nations, and cities in particular, to cope with increased urbanization, or it may take the form of the emergence of new kinds of solutions to the problems of both economic development and urbanization. However, these solutions are not yet on the horizon.

The paradox is that the same overurbanization can be viewed as either a major problem for newly developing countries or, from the long-range point of view—assuming appropriate and quick economic development—a major opportunity in the direction of rapid growth. At the moment there appears to be no really satisfactory measure for determining the existence, extent, and significance of overurbanization among many underdeveloped countries, although some measures are useful in specific cases. By no stretch of the imagination is overurbanization merely an academic question for responsible leaders of newly developing countries.

PROJECTIONS

Population projection is a professional and technical undertaking that is affected by a number of factors. First of all, the size of the population unit varies directly with the accuracy of the prediction: the larger the unit the more likely the projection will approximate the subsequent fact because of the cancellation of complicating factors and compensating errors. Reasonably reliable estimates have been made for future world population, less reliable estimates for major geographical regions, and even less reliable projections for countries and smaller sections of countries. Second, the obtaining of accurate data is hampered by the relative unreliability of census data from newly developing countries. And third, projections of population vary with the assumptions made in the process, including the rate at which population is expected to increase or decrease, the world political situation, the development of industrialization, and similar factors. Major variations in any one population factor or combination of factors will substantially influence the outcome of population projections. Therefore, considerable reservation should be attached to any projection for urbanization, particularly in newly developing countries.

Nevertheless, it is important to undertake projections for planning purposes and a number have accordingly been prepared. Among the most useful are those by Homer Hoyt in *World Urbanization,*[4] reproduced here as Tables 11, 12, and 13.

Table 11

World Population by Urban Size Groups: Estimated, 1960 and Projected for Years 1975 and 2000 *

Population Metropolitan Areas	1960	1975	2000	1960	1975	2000
	Millions			Per cent		
1,000,000 and over	285	496	1,285	9.6	13.0	20.5
500,000–999,000	88	181	465	3.0	4.7	7.4
300,000–499,000	66	143	355	2.2	3.7	5.7
100,000–299,000	151	257	539	5.1	6.7	8.6
Total 100,000 and over	590	1,077	2,644	19.9	28.1	42.2
Total cities and towns, 2,000–99,000	413	538	772	13.9	14.1	12.3
Total urban	1,003	1,615	3,416	33.9	42.2	54.5
Total rural	1,959	2,213	2,851	66.1	57.8	45.5
World total	2,962	3,828	6,267	100.0	100.0	100.0

* *Source:* Homer Hoyt, *World Urbanization: Expanding Population in a Shrinking World,* Urban Land Institute Technical Bulletin No. 43 (Washington, D.C.: Urban Land Institute, 1962), Table 17, p. 50.

As Hoyt points out in Table 11, projections for 1975 and 2000 indicate that by the year 2000 there will be almost as many people living in cities of 100,000 or more as are in the total world population at the present time. This represents an increase from an estimated 590 million persons living in places of 100,000 or more in 1960 to 2,644 million estimated to be living in these places by the year 2000, or an increase of 300 per cent. The corresponding percentages of the world population living in places of 100,000 or more between 1960 (19.9 per cent) and 2000 (42.2 per cent) indicate a world population increase of more than 100 per cent in places of 100,000 or more between 1960 and 2000.

Hoyt's estimate of the population of the world living in metropolitan areas of one million or more inhabitants indicates a shift of 9.6 per cent of the world population in such areas in 1960 to 20.5 per cent in 2000, or

[4] Homer Hoyt, *World Urbanization: Expanding Population in a Shrinking World,* Urban Land Institute Technical Bulletin No. 43 (Washington, D.C.: Urban Land Institute, 1962), Tables 17, 16, and 15, pp. 48–50.

Table 12

Percentage of World Population in Urban Areas by Size Group, and Rural Areas by Continents: 1960, 1975, and 2000 *

Continent	1,000,000 and over	500,000–999,000	300,000–499,000	100,000–299,000	100,000 and over	2,000 to 5,000–99,000	Rural areas and villages less than 2,000–5,000
	Per cent						
Year 1960							
North America[a]	34	9	6	11	60	24	16
Latin America[b]	12	4	3	6	25	20	55
Europe[c]	13	5	3	8	30	24	46
Asia	6	2	1	3	12	9	79
Africa	2	1	2	3	8	7	85
Oceania	25	6	6	6	44	19	37
World total	10	3	2	5	20	14	66
Year 1975							
North America[a]	35	9	6	10	60	25	15
Latin America[b]	20	6	5	8	39	16	45
Europe[c]	15	8	5	8	36	24	40
Asia	10	3	3	6	22	10	68
Africa	4	4	3	5	16	9	75
Oceania	25	12	6	7	50	10	40
World total	13	5	4	6	28	14	58
Year 2000							
North America[a]	40	12	10	15	77	13	10
Latin America[b]	25	8	7	10	50	10	40
Europe[c]	20	12	7	9	48	22	30
Asia	20	6	5	8	39	11	50
Africa	8	6	4	7	25	7	68
Oceania	27	13	8	7	55	10	35
World total	21	7	6	8	42	12	46

[a] North America, north of Mexico.
[b] North America, south of U.S.A., and all of South America.
[c] Including Asiatic portion of U.S.S.R.
* *Source:* Homer Hoyt, *World Urbanization: Expanding Population in a Shrinking World,* Urban Land Institute Technical Bulletin No. 43 (Washington, D.C.: Urban Land Institute, 1962), Table 16, p. 49.

a change from 285 million in 1960 to 1,285 million in 2000. Using each nation's official definition of urban, Hoyt anticipates that the 33.9 per cent defined as urban in 1960 will increase to 54.5 per cent in 2000. At the same time that the shift from, roughly, 1,000 million persons living in

Table 13

Estimated and Projected Urban Population by Size Groups, and Rural Population by Continents, 1960, 1975, and 2000 *

Continent	1,000,000 and over	500,000–999,000	300,000–499,000	100,000–299,000	100,000 and over	2,000 to 5,000–99,000	Rural areas and villages less than 2,000–5,000
				Millions			
Year 1960							
North America[a]	67	18	12	22	119	47	31
Latin America[b]	25	8	6	13	51	41	116
Europe[c]	80	35	21	53	189	152	298
Asia	102	25	22	55	204	151	1,296
Africa	6	2	4	8	20	18	213
Oceania	4	1	1	1	7	3	6
World total	284	89	66	152	590	412	1,960
Year 1975							
North America[a]	84	22	14	24	144	60	36
Latin America[b]	61	18	15	24	118	48	137
Europe[c]	113	60	38	60	271	180	300
Asia	221	66	66	133	486	221	1,503
Africa	12	12	9	15	48	27	228
Oceania	5	3	1	1	10	2	9
World total	496	181	143	257	1,077	538	2,213
Year 2000							
North America[a]	125	37	31	47	240	41	32
Latin America[b]	148	47	41	59	296	59	238
Europe[c]	189	114	66	85	454	208	284
Asia	774	232	194	310	1,509	425	1,935
Africa	41	31	21	36	129	36	352
Oceania	8	4	2	2	16	3	10
World total	1,285	465	355	539	2,644	772	2,851

[a] North America, north of Mexico.
[b] North America, south of U.S.A., and all of South America.
[c] Including Asiatic portion of U.S.S.R.
* *Source:* Homer Hoyt, *World Urbanization: Expanding Population in a Shrinking World,* Urban Land Institute Technical Bulletin No. 43 (Washington, D.C.: Urban Land Institute, 1962), Table 15, p. 48.

urban areas in 1960 to 3,416 million living in such places in 2000 is taking place, there will also be an increase in the rural population, the net result being that somewhat more than half of the world population will be living in urban areas by 2000.

Table 12 distributes the projection data by major continental area and city size group, showing the projections in terms of percentage; Table 13 gives the actual quantities involved. Although both these tables merit careful study, not all of the details can be commented upon here. It is interesting, however, to observe that in Latin America for places of one million or more population, the percentage increases from 12 in 1960 to an estimated 25 in 2000, more than 100 per cent, whereas in Asia—which had 6 per cent of its population living in such places in 1960—the estimated population increase to 20 per cent of its population in the year 2000 would be a 200 per cent increase. With reference to the percentage of the continental population living in places of 100,000 or more, in Latin America 25 per cent lived in such places in 1960; this percentage would double by 2000. The percentage in change would more than triple for Asia, from 12 per cent in 1960 to 39 per cent in 2000; and for Africa the change would be from 8 per cent in 1960 to 25 per cent in 2000. All of the above projections by Hoyt are based on the assumption that the world population will increase at the median rate predicted by the United Nations, and that there will be an increasing degree of industrialization throughout the world.

One of the implications of these enormous changes in population living in different size places and in different parts of the world was suggested in Table 10, which shows housing requirements from 1960 to 1975, as discussed in Chapter Four.

As has been indicated, there are variations in projections of population, depending upon the source of a projection. A variation from the one proposed by Hoyt was prepared by Philip M. Hauser, who observes that:

The rate of world urbanization, and particularly that of the areas with low proportions of urban population at the present time, may be expected to continue to accelerate. In 1950, about 502 million persons lived in cities of 20,000 and over. By 1975, should the rate of urbanization as observed between 1900 and 1950 continue and total world population increase in accordance with the United Nations projections, urban population in places of this size will have more than doubled, to reach a level of 1.2 billions. Similarly, under the same conditions, population in cities of 100,000 and over—314 million in 1950—could reach a level of 745 million, *i.e.*, also more than double, by 1975. Even if the proportion of the world's urban population remained fixed from 1950 to 1975, the population in places of 20,000 and over would increase by about 55 per cent simply because of total population increase alone. If the trend continues, by 1975 30 per cent of the world's people will live in cities of 20,000 and over, and 19 per cent will live in cities of 100,000 and over. The large share of the increase in the world's urban population will occur in the economically underdeveloped areas. Asia, alone, will account for over half the increase during the 1950 to 1975 period.[5]

These projections are somewhat more modest than those made by Hoyt, indicating the difficulty in arriving at an average projection for urbanization over long periods and for many different kinds of countries.

For illustrative purposes it may be helpful to examine urbanization projections for a particular part of the world. Such a case is offered by India. In 1962 Kingsley Davis presented tables showing the estimated size of ten major cities in India in 1970 and 2000. The figures were presented in terms of both low and high estimates. Assuming that the low estimates were on the conservative side, Davis suggested that if the present rates of increase continue, by 2000 Calcutta will have a population of 35.6 million, Delhi 17.8 million, Bombay 11.9 million, Madras 8.9 million, Bangalore 7.1 million, Ahmedabad and Hyderabad over 5 million each, Kanpur and Poona over 4 million each, and Nagpur 3.6 million. The high estimates were substantially greater, being respectively 66, 33, 22, 16.5, 13, 11, 9, 8, 7, and 6.6 million, or roughly twice the low estimates.[6] The implications of such urbanization are reserved for the speculation of the reader.

Without question, even the most conservative projections seem to indicate a massive urbanization in the future. It is likely that the next 50 years or less will duplicate or perhaps increase the present results of 6,000 years of physical development in urban areas. Just how this development will be duplicated, at what level of quality, and other matters remain to be considered, but the answers are likely to depend on the capacity of underdeveloped countries, in particular, to cope successfully with problems of economic development. The prospect is a large and almost ominous one, as Kingsley Davis has suggested, in terms of there eventually being possibly 85 to 95 per cent of the world population living in places of 5,000 or more and being involved in urban occupations, resulting in a situation "as urbanized as the most urban countries today." [7]

[5] Hauser, *op. cit.*, p. 201. See also Kingsley Davis, "The Urbanization of the Human Population," *Scientific American*, **213** (September 1965), 41–53, reprinted in *Cities* (New York: Alfred A. Knopf, Inc., 1965), pp. 3–24.

[6] See Kingsley Davis, "Urbanization in India: Past and Future," in Roy Turner, ed., *India's Urban Future* (Berkeley: University of California Press, 1962), pp. 20, 25. The potential for cities of such size and some of their implications are suggested by the discussion of Richard L. Meier, "Relations of Technology to the Design of Very Large Cities," in Turner, *op. cit.*, pp. 299ff. For further exploration of these topics by Meier, see his *Science and Economic Development: New Patterns of Living* (Cambridge, Mass.: Massachusetts Institute of Technology Press; and New York: John Wiley & Sons, Inc., 1956).

[7] Kingsley Davis, "Origin and Growth of Urbanization in the World," *American Journal of Sociology*, **40** (March 1955), 437.

IS THE PAST A PROLOGUE?

These projections of future urbanization raise the question as to whether the past is the prologue for the future. The answer cannot be precisely determined. Perhaps the past is likely to be the prologue for the future since there is no indication of any slackening of the move toward cities, in fact, quite the reverse. Moreover, many of the tortuous steps in the recent strong move toward urbanization will doubtless be repeated over and over, even though better methods are widely known, partly as a result of very rapid urban growth in situations where adequate provision cannot be made in advance. The continuing lack of physical and financial resources to cope with the scale of growth, inmigration, the scarcity of jobs, governmental inertia and incapacity to mount a broad and intensive program to cope with urbanization are some of the additional reasons for a continuation of the present trend toward urbanization.

On the other hand, the past may not be a prologue for the future if increased industrialization can improve the economic base, enlarge job opportunities, and expand productive capacity for goods to be used in the cities. There already exist an increasing amount of planning being undertaken, evidence of a deeper awareness of the urgency of urbanization-related problems among responsible leaders and governments, and more and more knowledge about how to produce housing at reasonable costs. Insofar as industrialization accompanies urbanization, there tends to be increased income and, therefore, greater capacity of the individual to make his own way in the city and, accordingly, produce additional revenue, one of the means by which the city can deal with its major problems. Therefore, we cannot say whether the past will be a prologue for the future, particularly in view of the fact that there is at the present time no way of knowing whether the present rates of urbanization in newly developing countries will continue, increase, or decrease, and where and under what circumstances.

The prospect is indeed uninviting, if not gloomy, for urbanization appears likely to continue at a pace in excess of economic development sufficient to cope with this urbanization. Philip M. Hauser, a long-time observer and student of the urbanization process in various parts of the world, notes that:

> It is very doubtful that, over this span of time, the underdeveloped nations can attain economic development of adequate dimensions to meet Western standards of living for their present and future city dwellers. The fundamental

economic objective of the underdeveloped areas is that of increasing productivity; and the many difficulties in meeting their efforts to attain this objective are likely to be exacerbated rather than ameliorated by present and prospective rapid rates of urban growth.[8]

This condition is likely to be accompanied among developing areas by the incapacity of its agriculture to stave off nationwide famine. The twentieth century "revolution of rising expectations" finds the public seeking a much higher standard of living than was available in the nineteenth century. The problem of increasing and maintaining agricultural productivity to support projected increases in total population, including the agricultural *surplus* necessary for urbanization, is extremely ominous. Even if agricultural production can be expanded, at the present time this expansion seems likely to take place on too small a scale and too late; at the very least there will probably be a massive decline in the dietary level of much of the world's population. Meeting the fiscal or financial problems of urbanization—a closely related problem which is directly related to the capacity of government to adapt itself to the new requirements of national economic growth and urbanization—also reflects the endlessly enlarging gap between the needs of urban areas and the capacity of urban residents to pay for them. As has been pointed out, "development without urbanism is an undesirable phenomenon, but there is no worse combination than urbanization without development, because to the lack of urban facilities is added the want of employment opportunities." [9]

Taking the above factors into account, the prospect is that the amenities so fondly imagined as associated with urbanism as a way of life are likely to become progressively more inaccessible for an increasingly large segment of the world population. These people may, in fact, have to revert to subsistence urbanization, a concept introduced earlier, or it may be that the shape of things to come will be *sub*-subsistence urbanization.

Differentials in the rate and extent of change of urbanization are to be expected. It may even be that some stages will be skipped. As Moore notes:

> It is evident that not all historic rates of change or even sequences must be recapitulated, partly because the products of the past become the ever richer inventory for the present, an inventory permitting some choice of items and combinations. Those products are social as well as economic, ideas as well as

[8] Hauser, *op. cit.,* p. 203.
[9] UNESCO, *Latin America,* p. 37.

goods. Yet functional connections and limits of resources certainly impose some restraints on choice and temporal priorities.[10]

If appropriate measures to solve the problems of economic development can be invented and applied in adequate proportion, it is possible that some of the more frightening prospects for urbanization in the near future may be ameliorated. If so, some of the questions regarding what will happen to the old culture and the old society in the course of urbanization, and what will happen to people, may be more readily answered than at present.

The evidence has not yet made it possible to determine an optimum rural-urban population balance in developing countries, or anywhere else. Further, it is not clear what patterns future urbanization will take. Since a considerable amount of caution must therefore be exercised, many countries are taking steps to decelerate urbanization.[11] Among these efforts are desperate attempts to increase agricultural productivity and income, make village life more attractive, stimulate village and cottage industry, decentralize new industrial development, improve communications, promote resettlement, reclamation, and irrigation programs, stimulate land tenure reform, and undertake national, regional, and city planning projects.

Pressure to improve existing urban areas is strong, but under present circumstances the resolution of urban problems might become self-defeating since it would make urban areas even more attractive to rural residents than before. Therefore, balanced development in urban and rural areas, no matter how difficult to achieve, is the only possible long-term solution.

One encouraging factor lies in a major difference between Western urbanization and urbanization in newly developing countries. Western urbanization was, by and large, haphazard and slow. This relatively slow rate of urbanization had the merit of allowing time for adaptation, for improvising, and even for planning for the provision and development of new tools of control such as zoning and the marshalling of resources to deal with urbanization. If they wish, newly developing countries can learn from the serious past mistakes of Western urbanization by intelligently planned urbanization. However, this is unlikely to happen unless substantially more attention is devoted to the matter than present evidence indicates.

[10] Wilbert E. Moore, Inter-American Sociology Seminar, Princeton University, September 1962, "Introduction: Social Change and Comparative Studies," *International Social Science Journal,* **15**, 4 (1963), 527.

[11] UNESCO, *Asia and the Far East,* p. 36; and UNESCO, *Latin America,* pp. 304ff.

Some of the policy implications of these developments have been suggested in UNESCO studies of urbanization in various parts of the world.[12]

THE CITY IS THE COUNTRY

In many newly developing countries the city *is* the country—it is the country's window to the world, in both directions. The outside world first gathers its impressions of a country's culture, capacities, achievements, nature, and importance from that country's cities. Compare, for example, the impression of India received by a visitor who first arrives in Calcutta with that of one whose first exposure to the country is New Delhi.

Furthermore, it is in the city that the inhabitants of a country get their first impression of the world outside their own, and of the viability and potential of their own country as exhibited in the urban showcase. Perhaps it is for this reason, among others, that the residents of newly developing countries have to be shown that: We, too, can build skyscrapers; we, too, can design modern architecture.

The inevitability of urbanization in newly developing countries—with more and more and larger and larger cities—will not occur in a vacuum, or be without profound consequences for society, and conversely. This process must be seen in a two-way context in which urbanization, on the one hand, and the economy, the society, and the culture on the other hand, are inextricably dependent on each other. Certainly it is true, for example, that it is in the cities that the political future of a country may well be determined. Here will be found the theater for the working out of the drama of nationhood. Is there not more than a resounding echo in the contention that, from here on in, whoever controls the cities controls the countries?

The imponderables of one time have a way of being resolved in a later one. This short study of urbanization in newly developing countries undergoing the process of modernization began with a short picture of a day in the life of a city.

How will the *new* new day begin . . . and end?

[12] See UNESCO, *Latin America,* pp. 294ff; UNESCO, *Asia and the Far East,* pp. 36ff; UNESCO, *Africa South of the Sahara;* United Nations Bureau of Social Affairs, *United Nations Seminar on Regional Planning,* Tokyo, July 28–August 8, 1958 (New York: United Nations, 1958); and a special issue on regional planning (Tokyo conference), *Housing, Building, and Planning,* Nos. 12 and 13 (United Nations, 1959).

INDEX